The Old Fashioned
Homemade Ice Cream Cookbook

The Old Fashioned

HOMEMADE

ICE CREAM

Cookbook

by Joyce & Christopher W. Dueker

The Bobbs-Merrill Company, Inc.

INDIANAPOLIS   NEW YORK

ISBN 0-672-51765-5
Library of Congress catalog card number 73-11803
Designed by Winston Potter
Manufactured in the United States of America

First printing

For Kenneth and Donna

"Purity is best demonstrated
by generosity."

Luke 11:41
*The Living Bible
Paraphrased*

Contents

Introduction

The proof of the pudding is in the eating.

—JOSEPH ADDISON

Listen carefully on a still, warm night and you may hear a strange creak-crank noise. Someone nearby is making ice cream!

What accounts for the recent revival of interest in homemade ice cream? Certainly, the proof is in the eating: no commercial ice cream can compare with the lightness and honest flavor of homemade ice cream.

When you make your own ice cream, you use no artificial flavorings, nor do you adulterate it with stabilizers or emulsifiers.

Beyond the consideration of taste goes the pure joy of creating. In this modern world of convenience foods, many people are returning to making their own breads, putting up their own preserves. And so you will discover a kind of creative pleasure in the process of mixing and freezing your own ice cream. Guests will marvel at your skill, notwithstanding your modest disclaimers.

Best of all, it is quite easy to make ice cream. The ingredients are readily available, and an ice cream freezer doesn't represent a major investment. Even the least experienced cook will find most of the recipes in this book well within his or her capability. It's a matter of a few minutes to mix up most flavors. Freezing, even with a hand crank model, then takes less than half an hour.

Nutritionally, ice cream has the strengths and weaknesses of all dairy foods. Like milk, it provides an excellent source of phosphorus, calcium, vitamin A, and the B vitamins—riboflavin and thiamine. Because of a higher fat content, it exceeds milk in the amount of thiamine. Ice cream can also be considered a good protein food.

Unfortunately, the good, rich taste of ice cream comes from a high fat content. In general, the finer the ice cream, the higher its milk fat percentage. A representative sample of ice cream has 400 calories per cup as compared to 200 calories for a cup of whole milk. Because of lower milk fat levels, ice milk and sherbet have fewer than 300 calories per cup. Water ices are fat-free and have only 150 calories per cup.

For persons who must limit their fat intake, sherbets are pleasant desserts. Water ices are even better. (Imitation ice cream provides no benefit for the dieter. Like imitation milk, it is made with coconut oil for "good" flavor, since vegetable oils, low in saturated fat, evidently give imitation milk and ice cream an unpleasant taste. Coconut oil is high in saturated fats, hence you gain nothing except money by eating imitation ice cream: you are eating the same number of calories with the same amount of fat.)

One of the nicest things about homemade ice cream is that you can skimp on fat and still make delicious desserts. Because you use superior flavorings and avoid fillers, you don't have to rely on richness for good taste. Try making ice cream with milk instead of cream: your fans will still declare it richer and better than higher fat commercial flavors. This holds true even when using skim milk.

I started making ice cream for my wife on our honeymoon because I recalled how good homemade ice cream had tasted on special occasions during childhood. Somewhat to my surprise I found the effort involved was minimal. It didn't take long to realize how much better mine tasted than average commercial ice cream.

The more my wife and I made homemade ice cream, the more we wanted. One day when we were sitting in Ed and Don's Ice Cream Parlor in Honolulu, Hawaii, my wife turned to me and said, ''Why don't we put together a book about homemade ice cream?'' That's how this book got its start.

The more we searched for recipes, the more it became obvious that most of the old ones were published with rather regal entertaining in mind. And too many of them included ingredients such as flour and gelatin.

My wife, who is more of a practical thinker than a researcher, turned to me and said, ''Put all those musty books away—we'll make up our own recipes.''

Thus, each of the recipes in this book is original. All of them were patiently tested until they achieved the best possible taste in the simplest way. Some (like vanilla) were easy to formulate, while others (like eggnog) required many tries before success came. The making of so much ice cream took its toll. I wore out two hand crank freezers. My wife complained bitterly about an additional five pounds, directly related to so much testing.

Nevertheless, we have found ice cream making a pleasurable pastime. We encourage you to give it a try. After all, no other food seems so festive, tastes so good, or brings more pleasure to creator and tester.

i

History
of Ice Cream

The emperor is emperor of ice cream.

—WALLACE STEVENS

Though ice cream is widely regarded as America's national dessert, its origin stretches back at least to the Roman Empire. Nero Claudius Caesar, Emperor of Rome, employed swift runners to bring him mountain snow, which was then flavored at his palace with fruit juices—the first water ices.

In the thirteenth century Marco Polo included recipes for frozen milk desserts among the treasures he brought back from China. From this beginning the idea of ice cream spread from Italy into France and from there to the English court. At that time, such a delicacy was felt to be unfit for the masses—Charles I of England is supposed to have had one of his French chefs executed for revealing the formula.

In the western hemisphere, Montezuma reportedly enjoyed ice cream in the period before Cortez. The first recorded evidence of ice cream in Colonial America appeared in a letter written after a dinner at the home of Governor Williams of Maryland in the early 1700s. Historians, with their passion for exactness, have revealed that such personages as George Washington, Alexander Hamilton and Dolly Madison enjoyed eating it. And among his manifold talents, Thomas Jefferson included ice cream making, a skill he learned while living in France.

The first ice cream parlors were opened in New York in the late eighteenth century. Through all this time ice cream had been frozen by hand by shaking a covered metal can contained in an ice-filled bucket. It was not until 1846 that Nancy Johnson devised a freezer using a crank and a dasher. Her invention made commercial ice cream production possible.

In 1851 Jacob Fussel spurred commercial development by founding the nation's first wholesale ice cream factory in Washington, D.C. In 1856 he added a Baltimore factory, and in 1864 he opened another in St. Louis.

From then on the popularity of ice cream grew unchecked. Technical advances included pasteurization in 1895 and homogenization in the early 1900s. The commercial freezing technique evolved from brine-cooled batch freezers to continuous freezers, which have been in use since 1930. Mass production has helped reduce the price from the $1.25 per quart charged by Jacob Fussel—a price worth much more in his day.

The ice cream soda was introduced at the Centennial Exposition in Philadelphia in 1879. The ice cream cone first made its dripping debut at the St. Louis World's Fair in 1904. Nobody knows exactly when or how the ice cream sundae was invented. A story in children's literature tells about a king whose cook

invented the first hot fudge sundae. This has been put
into verse as follows:

The new cook, George, was feeling bold;
He set before the King pie à la mode.
But the King was not happy and so roared,
"Take it away; it's cold!"

The next day George made turkey and gravy.
"What's this?" the King bellowed.
George said, "Turkey and gravy, beloved by your
Navy."
"Well," the King hissed, "it pleases me not—it's
hot!"

"Bring me something both hot and cold," the King
continued,
"Or I'll have your head on a platter."
Trembling and tripping, George dashed to the
kitchen.
He consulted all his books in vain, then made up
something new.

"What's this?" the King asked.
"Something hot: something cold," George said.
"Why, then, I'll try it," the King wheezed,
And took a huge bite of the hot fudge sundae.
"With this," the King said, "I am pleased."

Although no longer the purview of royalty, ice
cream certainly has not fallen in popularity. Ameri-
cans eat more than 500 million gallons each year. No
wonder then that *Gourmet* calls ice cream "America's
favorite dessert."

Ice cream has many cousins in the frozen dessert

family. Some of these closely resemble ice cream, while others are similar only in that they are frozen. Desserts similar to ice cream include mousses and parfaits. These have similar ingredients but are frozen without stirring. Unfortunately for the cause of clarity, ''parfait'' also describes an ice cream sundae served in a tall glass. Similarly, a frappé can be either a semifrozen sherbet or an ice cream milk shake.

Water ices are the simplest of the frozen desserts; they are made from water, fruit flavorings and sugar. They are not a dairy product.

ii

Techniques for Making Ice Cream

There is no burthen so heavy which being
sustained by many, becometh not light.
—STEFANO GUAZZO

Friends often comment that it must be hard to make ice cream. Truthfully, it is easy with the new equipment and the simple techniques involved. Follow these simple instructions and your first batch and all to follow will be successful.

THE EQUIPMENT

The ice cream freezer and how it works: The ice cream freezer does more than just turn the liquid mix into a solid—it gives the light texture which distinguishes ice cream from simple frozen cream. Ice cream can be frozen in the refrigerator freezer, but unless stirred it turns out heavy and crystalline. Ice cream freezers solve this problem by stirring the mix constantly during the freezing process, to make it light and fluffy.

The ice cream mix is put into a metal can that fits into the center of the freezer, with space around it for the ice. A dasher is fitted into it before the top is put on. Then the can is packed around with ice (in fact a mixture of ice and rock salt, as you will see below), and a hand crank is attached to the outside of the freezer. This fits onto the ice cream can inside and slowly turns it. Inside the can the dasher remains stationary as the can moves around it (just the opposite of beating eggs in a bowl)—in effect scraping the quickly formed crystals from the cold sides of the can and distributing them through the mix until all is evenly frozen. Thus the ice cream is stirred within the can while being chilled by the ice-and-salt mix outside it, smoothing the texture while reducing the time required for freezing.

So to become a good ice cream maker, you will first need a trusty ice cream freezer.

Selecting your ice cream freezer: Home ice cream freezers are not hard to find. They are well worth their moderate cost, $15 to $40, depending on whether you select a manual or electric model. These can be found in most large hardware or department stores. Unless you live in a perpetually warm area like Hawaii, you'll have an easier time finding a freezer in the spring or in the summer. Two of the many nationwide sources are Sears, Roebuck and J. C. Penney Company.

If you have a choice of sizes, we suggest selecting the largest home freezer available. With a large ice cream freezer you're all set for a party, yet it can easily be used to make smaller quantities.

We prefer the hand-powered models over the electric

motor-driven freezers. Outside of the significant cost
difference, there is the advantage of greater port-
ability. And somehow ice cream seems more homemade
when it's hand cranked, even if an objective observer
finds the tastes identical. Hand cranking is not at all
difficult, and bystanders are eager to give it a try—
after all, the cranker gets to lick the dasher.

With reasonable care a freezer will last a long time.
But note that the ice-and-rock-salt brine is corrosive,
so all exposed metal parts should be cleaned and dried
after each use. The container should be completely
washed and scalded also.

Ice and rock salt: To freeze ice cream you will need
a supply of ice and rock salt. Ice alone is not so efficient
a cooling agent as a brine made of ice and rock salt.
Water normally turns into ice at 32 degrees Fahrenheit. Adding salt to the ice lowers its freezing point—
a temperature of 16 to 18 degrees Fahrenheit can
easily be maintained in salt and ice. This phenomenon
explains why salt is used to melt ice on roads and side-
walks. Obviously this lower temperature hastens the
freezing of the ice cream.

What to buy: For freezing ice cream you should
buy a coarse-grained salt labeled "rock salt" or "ice
cream salt." This can be found in most markets.

Proportion of ice to rock salt: This is important:
Eight parts of ice to one part of rock salt works best.
A higher salt content will speed up the freezing, but
in home freezers this will result in a granular ice
cream. Too little salt will unnecessarily prolong the
freezing process.

Quantity of ice needed: It takes about four refrigerator trays of ice to freeze one quart of ice cream. Be sure that you have plenty of ice on hand before you start: nothing spoils the fun like running out of ice halfway through the cranking.

How to prepare the ice: Crushed ice works best since it provides more surface area for heat exchange. Put ice cubes or chips in a burlap bag and crush them with a mallet or a sturdy rock. This should be done the last minute. (Instructions on how to pack the freezer with the crushed ice and rock will be found on page 21.)

THE INGREDIENTS

Homemade ice cream has three basic ingredients: cream, a sweetener and flavoring.

The cream: Your choice of cream will determine the richness of the ice cream and therefore its calorie content.

Naturally, heavy whipping cream with about 35% butterfat content makes the richest ice cream; however, it is very expensive, high in calories, and really too rich for most tastes. Light cream, with 20% butterfat content, would be a good compromise. We prefer Half and Half, which has 12% butterfat, since it gives a good richness without being overly fattening. When we want richer ice cream, we simply combine Half and Half with heavy whipping cream, using equal amounts of each. This makes a highly satisfactory ice cream.

The sweetener: For sweetening, we use only granulated sugar. Corn sugar or artificial sweeteners can be used, but they'll modify the flavor unpleasantly.

The flavoring: In flavor, homemade ice cream has no peer. Whether you use extract, nuts, fruits, chocolate, or coffee, the genuineness of the flavor will be apparent. Don't scrimp on the quality of your flavoring. A little goes a long way, and you will be able to taste the difference—all of your ice cream will taste different from the corresponding commercial flavor. This is most noticeably true for sherbets and simply points out the difference between true and artificial flavorings. You will find, for the most part, that homemade ice cream flavors are lighter and more delicate—compare the tastes of your homemade orange sherbet and a commercial one, and see the difference.

Also, the color of your homemade ice cream may be different from what you expected. For example, pistachio nuts aren't really green. We have noted those ice creams that require artificial coloring (use pure vegetable dyes) to produce the expected color. After all, who really wants to eat white Lime Sherbet?

HOW TO MIX THE ICE CREAM

Scalding: With many ice creams, the cream requires scalding. The process of scalding concentrates the solids slightly and where indicated improves the flavor.

To scald cream (or Half and Half, or milk), heat it slowly in a saucepan until just below the boiling point, when small bubbles begin to appear around the edges of the saucepan. Stir it for a minute or two, watching closely to avoid boiling, then take it off the fire and cool. (Scalded cream will have a thin coating on it, but this disappears during cranking.)

Adding the sugar: Sugar will dissolve more easily if added before the scalded cream has completely cooled. Excessive amounts of sugar retard freezing.

Adding the flavoring: With few exceptions (which will be noted), *flavorings should be added after the cream has cooled completely.*

Extracts (such as vanilla) and liquors have alcohol bases that would be altered in flavor by heating. These are added as soon as the cream is cool.

Fruits and nuts lower the freezing point of the mix. Therefore, to make freezing faster, fruits and nuts are added at a later stage—when the ice cream has been frozen to a semisoft state, i.e., after cranking. Fruits and nuts also complicate the cranking process by sticking to the dasher.

Chilling the mix: After flavoring has been added to the cooled cream, the mix should be put into a bowl and set in the refrigerator until thoroughly chilled (an hour or two). The freezer can also be prechilled in the refrigerator or in ice water at this time.

HOW TO FREEZE
THE ICE CREAM

When the ice cream mix is chilled, crack your ice as directed on page 18 and have it ready along with the rock salt. Remember that you'll need about four refrigerator trays of ice to freeze one quart of ice cream, so be sure you have enough.

How to fill the freezer can: Take the prechilled freezer can out of the refrigerator, along with the chilled ice cream mix, and pour the mix into the can. *Fill it no more than three-quarters full* to allow room for the ice cream to expand. (Your homemade ice cream will expand only about 25%, as opposed to commercial ice cream, which doubles in volume.)

Insert the dasher and put on the top of the freezer can. Place the can securely in the freezer.

How to pack the ice and rock salt: As soon as the ice cream can is in the freezer, pack a two-inch layer of crushed ice on the bottom of the freezer all around it. Follow this with about a quarter-inch layer of the rock salt. Then repeat the layers until the ice/rock salt is up above the level of the ice cream mix in the can. Work fast, and don't layer up too high, or the brine may seep in at the top and spoil your ice cream. Attach the crank to the freezer and you're ready to start cranking.

How to crank: As soon as the ice and rock salt are packed in, start cranking. Start out fairly slowly, keeping the can going gently around in the brine. About sixty revolutions per minute is good at this stage. (Don't start out by cranking too fast: in addition to wearing yourself out, you'll actually retard the freezing by causing frictional heat.)

As the ice melts, you should replace it. Excess water can be poured off or allowed to drain out through the freezer's bung hole.

Do not stop cranking for more than a few seconds or a frozen crust will form between the dasher blades and the can wall, immobilizing the can. This is also why you must begin cranking right after the ice is in.

You can gradually increase your cranking tempo as the ice cream begins to freeze.

It takes about fifteen to twenty minutes to freeze a quart of ice cream. You are done when the crank is hard to turn and the ice cream has the consistency of stiffly whipped cream. Continued cranking will not make the ice cream harder, and it can damage the mechanism of the freezer. Further, if you're working with rich cream, you can easily produce small lumps of butter!

Remove the crank and the freezer can top, being careful not to spill the brine inside. Pull out the dasher and either lick it or scrape the adhering ice cream into the can.

Adding the final flavorings: This is the proper time to stir in additional flavorings such as fruits and nuts or crushed candy.

To harden the ice cream: Put the covered can in your refrigerator freezer, or transfer the semifrozen ice cream to a loaf pan or freezer dishes. Work quickly, because homemade ice cream melts rapidly. *Hardening will take about two to three hours in an efficient refrigerator freezer.*

Alternatively, you can harden it back in the ice cream freezer. First seal up the dasher hole in the can top. Then pour out the melted ice and replace the sealed can inside the freezer. Repack ice and salt around the can within the freezer, as before. Here a higher proportion of rock salt (four of ice to one of rock salt) should be employed to give faster freezing. Cover the freezer with newspapers or a towel and place it in a shady area. The ice cream will be hard enough for serving within one to two hours. Note that homemade ice cream freezes to a harder state than the commercial, since homemade contains less air and no emulsifiers or stabilizers.

Ripening and keeping: Homemade ice creams, especially fruit flavors, will improve if they are allowed to "ripen" overnight. Theoretically, homemade ice cream will keep well for several weeks. However, after prolonged storage its texture becomes coarse, so for maximum smoothness serve your ice cream pronto. Remember that homemade ice cream does not have emulsifiers and stabilizers, so it will never keep as well as commercial ice cream.

iii

Versatile Vanilla Ice Cream

Life is like an ice cream cone;
you have to learn to lick it.
—CHARLES SCHULZ

Vanilla provides the best introduction to the joys of homemade ice cream, for it is the simplest flavor—although a striking one—and will demonstrate at once the superiority of homemade ice cream. For a real education, make your own and notice the spirited flavor that will stand alone—a hearty dessert not requiring any adornment.

There are three major types of vanilla ice cream: Philadelphia, custard and French.

Philadelphia ice cream contains only cream, sugar and flavoring. Its definition goes back to the 1800s when a Mrs. Lincoln writing in *The American Kitchen* explained that the term "Philadelphia ice cream" referred to ice creams made without eggs.

Custard ice cream, as might be guessed, has a custard base of eggs and flour. Since we find the idea of putting flour into ice cream abhorrent, we have never attempted it.

French vanilla ice cream contains egg yolks but, mercifully, no flour. Frequently, French vanilla is thought of as the richest of the vanillas, but the classical French recipe calls for milk and cream rather than the pure cream of the Philadelphia vanilla recipe.

After selecting the kind of vanilla ice cream you wish to make, you must decide how to flavor it. The simplest way is to use vanilla extract: this is quite satisfactory. Be sure to get *pure* vanilla extract. The slightly cheaper flavorings using synthetic vanilla should be avoided—why go to the effort of making your own ice cream and then impair the result with inferior ingredients?

For the ultimate flavor, use fresh vanilla beans. These long brown beans can be found in most supermarkets. Vanilla beans cost from $5 to $20 per pound, but a single lightweight bean goes a long way. The whole bean can be cooked with the cream and then removed to be reused several times. Another way to use the bean is to slit the pod, pouring the seeds into the cream as it heats. This depletes your bean supply more quickly, but it does make the flavor stronger, and the tiny seeds look appealing in the finished product.

Vanilla bean ice cream turns out a dazzling almost snow-white color.

All the recipes that follow make approximately one quart of ice cream, to serve four to six persons.

Philadelphia Vanilla Ice Cream

1 quart Half and Half
¾ cup sugar
A few grains of salt
1½ tablespoons pure vanilla extract,
or the seeds from 3 inches of
vanilla bean

Scald the Half and Half as directed on page 19. Remove from heat. If using vanilla bean, it should be added during the scalding. Add sugar and salt to the warm Half and Half and stir well. If using vanilla extract, add it only after the mix has cooled to avoid altering the alcohol-based flavor.

Chill in the refrigerator, then transfer to the ice cream freezer can. Crank and freeze as directed in Chapter II.

French Vanilla Ice Cream

This flavor appeals to many, but we think the egg taste dilutes the fresh, delicate taste of the vanilla.

1 pint milk
½ cup sugar
A pinch salt
4 egg yolks
1 tablespoon pure vanilla extract or
the seeds from 3 inches of vanilla
bean
1 cup heavy cream

Mix the milk, sugar, salt and egg yolks. Cook very slowly until the mixture has thickened. This takes about 20 minutes and results in a curdled mess. Do not fret over small lumps, as they disappear during cranking. If using vanilla bean, it should be added during the cooking.

During the cooking you must pay close attention and stir frequently to prevent burning. If you have a short attention span, heat the mixture over boiling water.

Cool the mixture, and if you are using vanilla extract, stir it in now along with the cup of heavy cream. Chill, crank and freeze as directed in Chapter II.

Philadelphia Vanilla Variations

The basic Philadelphia Vanilla Ice Cream recipe can easily be modified to create a wide variety of delicious flavors. The simplest technique is to add chopped candy or nuts: try chopping up a peppermint stick or almonds, or one of the following:

Chocolate Chip Ice Cream

To one quart of cooled Philadelphia Vanilla Ice Cream, add about ¾ cup chopped chocolate. For simplicity, use a package of chocolate chips. Or, if you wish, you can chip up a block of semisweet or sweetened cooking chocolate. Chill, crank and freeze as directed in Chapter II.

Butterscotch Chip Ice Cream

Just use butterscotch chips and proceed as in the preceding Chocolate Chip recipe.

Raisin-Nut Ice Cream

Make Philadelphia Vanilla Ice Cream as directed on page 29. As soon as the cranking is finished, mix in ⅓ cup of raisins and ⅓ cup of chopped walnuts. Then continue freezing as directed in Chapter II.

Vanilla Fudge Ribbon Ice Cream

The technique of ribboning requires a bit of practice. For best results use Emperor's Fudge Sauce.

1 recipe Emperor's Fudge Sauce
1 recipe Vanilla Ice Cream

First make the Emperor's Fudge Sauce.

Make a quart of Philadelphia or French Vanilla Ice Cream. As soon as the cranking is finished, transfer the ice cream to a loaf pan and place in the freezer unit of your refrigerator to harden as directed in Chapter II.

Ribboning:

When the ice cream is just short of being hard, pour strips of warm (not hot) fudge sauce over the top and cut it in gently with a knife. The ice cream

must be nearly hard and the sauce thick, or you'll
end up with chocolate ice cream! Only experience
can teach you when the ice cream has reached the
right consistency. Put it back into the freezer to
complete hardening.

Ken's Blue Ribbon Vanilla Sundae Ice Cream

Follow the recipe for Vanilla Fudge Ribbon Ice
Cream. Right after cranking, mix about ¼ cup
Spanish peanuts into the vanilla ice cream. Then
ribbon in Emperor's Fudge Sauce as above.

Vanilla Butterscotch Ribbon Ice Cream

Use the ribbon technique with Vanilla Ice Cream
and the Easy Butterscotch Sauce.

The technique of ribboning may also be used with
the fruit sauces or coffee syrup recipe of Chapter XII,
provided these are made sufficiently thick. These
recipes by no means exhaust the possibilities of combinations with vanilla ice cream. Try your own ideas.
Vanilla is a good mixer!

iv

Chocolate Ice Cream

Chewing the food of sweet and bitter fancy.
—WILLIAM SHAKESPEARE

Chocolate ice cream ranks second in commercial ice cream sales. However, when you taste your first batch of homemade chocolate ice cream, you will feel that you have discovered an entirely new flavor.

All the recipes that follow make approximately one quart of ice cream, to serve four to six persons.

Basic Chocolate Ice Cream

    1 **cup sugar**
       A few grains of salt
  ¼ **cup water**
    2 **squares (2 ounces) unsweetened chocolate**
    1 **quart Half and Half**
    2 **teaspoons pure vanilla extract**

Dissolve the sugar and salt in the water in the top of a double boiler over boiling water. Add the chocolate and continue heating while stirring until the chocolate has completely melted. Gradually stir in the Half and Half, and heat until it's scalded as directed in Chapter II.

Remove from heat and cool. Add vanilla extract, and chill, crank and freeze as directed in Chapter II.

Easy Chocolate Ice Cream

This is made merely by combining chocolate sauce with a vanilla ice cream mix. The only drawback is that the sauce tends to settle out in a puddle at the bottom of the container during storage. To avoid this, mix in the sauce very well, and be careful not to let the ice cream soften too much at any stage in the freezing.

> 1 **cup Emperor's Fudge Sauce**
> 1 **quart Half and Half**
> ¾ **cup sugar**
>   **A few grains of salt**
> 1 **tablespoon pure vanilla extract**

First make the Emperor's Fudge Sauce, then put it into a saucepan and stir in the Half and Half. Scald as directed in Chapter II, stirring continually until smoothly blended. Remove from heat and add the sugar and salt, stirring until dissolved. Cool, stir in the vanilla extract, and chill, crank and freeze as directed in Chapter II.

Chocolate Fudge Ice Cream

True chocolate lovers will be satisfied by this rich fudge flavor.

1½ cups sugar
A few grains of salt
½ cup water
6 squares (6 ounces) unsweetened chocolate
1 quart Half and Half
1 teaspoon pure vanilla extract

Dissolve the sugar and salt in the ½ cup water in the top of a double boiler over boiling water. Add the chocolate and stir well as it melts. Pour in the Half and Half, scalding the entire mixture as directed in Chapter II.

With this quantity of chocolate, thorough stirring will be necessary to avoid lumps. To be on the safe side, you may wish to strain the mix after scalding.

Cool, then stir in the vanilla extract. Chill, crank and freeze as directed in Chapter II.

Mexican Chocolate Ice Cream

In this recipe a subtle cinnamon taste combines with rich chocolate. An excellent surprise flavor for dinner parties!

A few grains of salt
1 cup sugar
¼ cup water
2 squares (2 ounces) unsweetened chocolate
2 sticks of cinnamon
1 quart Half and Half

Use a double boiler to heat the salt, sugar and water. Add the chocolate and cinnamon, stirring while this melts. When melted, stir in the Half and Half. Scald as directed in Chapter II, then remove the cinnamon sticks.

Chill, crank and freeze as directed in Chapter II.

Bittersweet Chocolate Ice Cream I

This recipe requires a lot of chocolate. But what a treat!

½ cup sugar
   A few grains of salt
½ cup water
8 squares (8 ounces) semisweet chocolate
1 quart Half and Half
1 teaspoon pure vanilla extract

Dissolve the sugar and salt in the water in the top of a double boiler. Add the chocolate and slowly melt. Stir in the Half and Half and scald as directed in Chapter II. For maximum smoothness, strain the mixture after scalding.

Chill. Add the vanilla extract. Crank and freeze as directed in Chapter II.

Bittersweet Chocolate Ice Cream II

If you have unsweetened chocolate on hand, try this.

> 1 **cup sugar**
> **A few grains of salt**
> ¼ **cup water**
> 4 **squares (4 ounces) unsweetened chocolate**
> 1 **quart Half and Half**
> 2 **teaspoons pure vanilla extract**

Cook as directed for Bittersweet Chocolate Ice Cream I.

Serendipity Chocolate-Chip Ice Cream

Make any chocolate ice cream as directed. Immediately after cranking, simply stir in ½ cup of chopped chocolate or chocolate chips and continue freezing as directed in Chapter II.

Rocky Road Ice Cream

Make any chocolate ice cream as directed. Immediately after cranking, add ⅓ cup of chopped walnuts and ⅓ cup of marshmallow bits and complete freezing as directed in Chapter II.

Chocolate Raisin or Chocolate Raisin Nut Ice Cream

Make any chocolate ice cream as directed. Immediately after cranking, stir in ⅓ cup of raisins. Add ⅓ cup of chopped walnuts if you wish to make Chocolate Raisin Nut. Complete freezing as directed in Chapter II.

Chocolate Coconut Ice Cream

Make any chocolate ice cream as directed. Immediately after cranking, stir in ¼ cup of shredded coconut. Then continue freezing as directed in Chapter II.

Chocolate Fudge Ribbon Ice Cream

1 recipe Emperor's Fudge Sauce
1 recipe Chocolate Ice Cream

First make the Emperor's Fudge Sauce.

Make any Chocolate Ice Cream, put into a loaf pan after cranking, and freeze as usual. When it is just short of hard, cut in the warm fudge sauce, following the directions for ribboning in Chapter II. Complete freezing.

Your children no doubt will give you ideas for even more variations.

Coffee Ice Cream

Perhaps you recall the cartoon in which one boy confided to another, "I just can't face the day until I've had my first coffee ice cream cone." You don't have to be a coffee drinker to appreciate the good taste of coffee ice cream.

You may approach it in several ways. You can use your own brewed coffee—we prefer Hawaiian Kona coffee, which to us has the best taste. After numerous experiments we found it simplest and most satisfactory to use instant coffee straight from the jar. Instant coffee works well because it dissolves neatly, permitting easy alterations in strength. If you taste the mix before freezing it, don't forget that aging will strengthen the flavor: beware of making it too strong, too early. Instant espresso coffee gives a strong flavor many people enjoy. Hint: you can increase the eye appeal of your coffee ice cream by sprinkling a few coffee bean fragments over the frozen surface.

All the recipes that follow make approximately one quart of ice cream, to serve four to six persons.

Basic Coffee Ice Cream I

> 2 tablespoons instant coffee
> 1 quart Half and Half
> ¾ cup sugar (or 6 tablespoons, if preferred)
> A few grains of salt
> 2 teaspoons pure vanilla extract

Add the instant coffee to the Half and Half and scald as directed in Chapter II, while stirring well. Add the sugar and salt, then cool before adding the vanilla extract. Heating the coffee enhances its flavor. True coffee aficionados may prefer a stronger coffee taste; this may be obtained by reducing the sugar to 6 tablespoons. After chilling, crank and freeze as directed in Chapter II.

Basic Coffee Ice Cream II

This is made with brewed coffee instead of instant. If you prefer, you may use leftover coffee, an economical method in a coffee-drinking household. Or, if you are the type who really likes to do it from the ground up, use ground coffee or whole roasted beans. In either case you must strain the mix before freezing it. Note that if you use whole beans the ice cream will be almost pure white instead of the usual light tan.

¾ cup brewed coffee (or ⅔ cup fresh-
  ground coffee or 2 cups whole coffee
  beans)
1 quart Half and Half
¾ cup sugar
  A few grains of salt
2 teaspoons pure vanilla extract

Brew the coffee, then slowly scald it with the Half
and Half as directed in Chapter II, stirring well. (Or
scald the Half and Half with the fresh-ground coffee
or with the whole coffee beans.) Add the sugar and
salt, and cool. (Strain if you have used ground coffee
or coffee beans.) When cool add the vanilla extract.
Chill, crank and freeze as directed in Chapter II.

Espresso Ice Cream

Instant espresso coffee makes a delicious, strongly
flavored ice cream.

1 quart Half and Half
2 tablespoons instant espresso coffee
½ cup sugar

Heat the Half and Half in a saucepan, stirring in
the instant espresso coffee, and scald as directed in
Chapter II. The coffee will dissolve easily with
moderate stirring. Remove from heat, add the sugar
and cool. Chill, crank and freeze as directed in
Chapter II.

Mocha Ice Cream I

This combines the flavor of chocolate with that of coffee. In this variation, coffee dominates the chocolate. We recommend it highly.

2 squares (2 ounces) semisweet chocolate
1 recipe Basic Coffee Ice Cream I

Simply add the semisweet chocolate to the Half and Half along with the instant coffee of Basic Coffee Ice Cream I. Heat slowly, stirring constantly, until the coffee and chocolate blend in completely. Then complete the recipe as directed.

Mocha Ice Cream II

If you like chocolate to dominate, use this version.

1 quart Half and Half
8 teaspoons instant coffee
¾ cup unsweetened cocoa powder
½ cup sugar
A pinch of salt
2 teaspoons pure vanilla extract

Scald the Half and Half with the instant coffee and the cocoa as directed in Chapter II, stirring well. Add sugar and salt. Cool, then add the vanilla extract. Chill, crank and freeze as directed in Chapter II.

Joyce's Coffee Fudge Ribbon Ice Cream

Try this at a party and be prepared for lots of compliments. Words fail to describe this exquisite flavor.

¼ cup Emperor's Fudge Sauce
1 quart Half and Half
2 tablespoons instant coffee
⅜ cup sugar
A few grains of salt
2 teaspoons pure vanilla extract
½ cup toasted almonds

First make the Emperor's Fudge Sauce.

Scald the Half and Half with the instant coffee as directed in Chapter II. Stir in the sugar and salt until dissolved. Cool, then add the vanilla extract. Chill, then crank as directed in Chapter II. Toast ½ cup chopped almonds by heating them on a cookie sheet in a 350-degree oven for 10 minutes, then stir them into the cream after cranking. Transfer to a loaf pan and continue freezing until the cream has almost hardened. Then cut in the warm fudge sauce, following the directions for making ribbon ice cream (page 31). Complete freezing.

Coffee Chocolate Chip Ice Cream

Make any coffee ice cream as directed. Immediately after cranking, stir in ½ cup of chopped chocolate pieces, or the same amount of chocolate chips. Complete freezing as directed in Chapter II.

vi

Old Standards

It is hard to teach an old dog new tricks.
—WILLIAM CAMDEN

Here you will find some familiar ice cream flavors, some of which you can find at the corner supermarket; if you make them at home, they'll be far superior to those you can buy.

All the recipes that follow make approximately one quart, to serve four to six persons.

Myrtle's Butter Brickle Ice Cream

This combines candy and ice cream making. Fortunately, it is easy to make the candy, and by now you are an old hand at making ice cream.

THE CANDY:

1 cup sugar
¼ cup butter
¼ cup chopped walnuts

Mix the sugar and butter in a sturdy saucepan and heat over a moderate fire until the sugar melts into a brown syrup (about 15 minutes). *Stir frequently to avoid burning the butter.*

Pour the hot sugar syrup into a buttered shallow pan, add the chopped nuts and set in the refrigerator to harden. When hard, crush. Do this by covering the pan with waxed paper and then hammering until the pieces are as small as you can make them. (Don't use the blender for this, or you'll get a fine powder. You want the crunchiness of small bits.) Set aside.

THE ICE CREAM:

1 quart Half and Half
¾ cup sugar
A few grains of salt
2 teaspoons pure vanilla extract

Scald the Half and Half as directed in Chapter II. Add the sugar and salt. Cool. Add the vanilla extract, then chill, crank and freeze as directed in Chapter II. When partially frozen, stir in the crushed candy. Complete freezing as directed in Chapter II.

Praline Ice Cream

THE PRALINE:

> 1 **cup sugar**
> ¾ **cup chopped pecans**

Slowly heat the sugar in a heavy skillet until it melts and forms a brown syrup. This requires 10 to 15 minutes of stirring. Then mix in the chopped nuts and set in the refrigerator to harden. When hard, crush as directed on page 52 and set aside.

THE ICE CREAM:

> 1 **quart Half and Half**
> ½ **cup sugar**
> **A few grains of salt**
> 2 **teaspoons pure almond extract**

Scald the Half and Half as directed in Chapter II and add the sugar and salt. Cool. Add the almond extract, then chill and crank as directed in Chapter II. Immediately after cranking, add the crushed praline and complete the freezing as directed in Chapter II. (Don't let the praline stand too long in the mushy cream, or the sugar will dissolve, leaving you with very sweet ice cream with nuts!)

Sid's Butterscotch Ice Cream

    2 tablespoons butter (don't substitute)
    ¾ cup brown sugar
    1 quart Half and Half
      A few grains of salt
    1½ teaspoons pure vanilla extract

Slowly melt the butter and sugar together in a saucepan, and stir well while gently cooking for about 10 minutes, or until the sugar melts into a brown syrup. Set aside to cool. Scald the Half and Half as directed in Chapter II. Remove from fire and when it is lukewarm stir it into the cooled brown sugar syrup. Cool, then add the salt and vanilla extract. Chill, crank and freeze as directed in Chapter II.

Quick Butterscotch Ice Cream

An easy way to make a super-rich butterscotch ice cream.

    12 ounces packaged butterscotch chips
    ½ cup water
    1 quart Half and Half
    1 teaspoon pure vanilla extract

Heat the butterscotch chips and water in the top of a double boiler over boiling water, stirring well. When the chips have melted, stir in the Half and Half, continuing to cook until scalded, as directed in

Chapter II. Remove from heat and allow to cool before adding the vanilla extract.

Chill, crank and freeze as directed in Chapter II.

Butterscotch Ribbon Ice Cream

Real butterscotch nuts will love this—it is about the most butterscotch you can get.

1 recipe Easy Butterscotch Sauce
1 recipe Quick Butterscotch Ice Cream

First make the Easy Butterscotch Sauce. Then make Quick Butterscotch Ice Cream. Transfer to a loaf pan, and when it is just short of hard, cut in the warm butterscotch sauce, following the directions for ribboning on page 31. Then freeze hard.

Butterscotch Chip Ice Cream

Make Quick Butterscotch Ice Cream. Chop up an additional ⅔ cup of packaged butterscotch chips and stir into the butterscotch ice cream immediately after the cranking. Then complete the freezing as directed in Chapter II.

Caramel Ice Cream

2 tablespoons butter
¾ cup sugar
1 quart Half and Half
2 teaspoons pure vanilla extract
A few grains of salt

Slowly melt the butter and sugar together in a saucepan, stirring continuously, until the sugar melts into a brownish syrup. Take off the fire and set aside to cool.

Scald the Half and Half as directed in Chapter II, then stir in the warm sugar syrup. This commonly produces a big ball of hard candy rather than the desired smooth texture. Don't despair. Just stir sturdily as you continue to heat the Half and Half, and the lump will dissolve. Cool, then add the vanilla extract and salt. Chill, crank and freeze as directed in Chapter II.

Caramel Fudge Ribbon Ice Cream

Make one recipe of Emperor's Fudge Sauce (page 31).

Then make Caramel Ice Cream as directed. Transfer to a loaf pan and freeze as usual. When it is just short of hard, cut in the warm fudge sauce, following the directions for ribboning on page 31.

Chopped nuts could provide an interesting addition, and should be added just after cranking. Freeze hard.

Burnt Almond Ice Cream

Make Caramel Ice Cream as directed.

Toast ½ cup of chopped almonds by heating them on a cookie sheet for 10 minutes in a 350-degree oven. Stir the almonds into the Caramel Ice Cream just after cranking, then complete freezing as directed in Chapter II.

Peanut Butter Ice Cream

This unusual ice cream tastes like frozen peanut butter. Dedicated peanut butter fans will love it. (Would you believe a peanut butter ice cream sandwich?)

1 **quart Half and Half**
1 **cup chunk-style peanut butter**
1 **cup sugar**
2 **teaspoons pure vanilla extract**

Mix the Half and Half and peanut butter in a saucepan and heat slowly, scalding as directed in Chapter II. Add the sugar and stir to dissolve. Cool. Add the vanilla extract, then chill, crank and freeze as directed in Chapter II.

Mint Ice Cream

If you like the taste of mint, this will hit the spot.

1 **quart Half and Half**
1 **cup sugar**
  A few grains of salt
1 **teaspoon pure vanilla extract**
2 **teaspoons peppermint extract**
  A few drops of green food coloring

Scald the Half and Half, then add the sugar and salt. Cool. Now add the vanilla and peppermint extracts. (Warning: don't use mint extract. It gives a horrid medicinal spearmint taste.) Stir in a few drops of green food coloring, then chill, crank and freeze as directed in Chapter II.

Mint Chocolate Chip Ice Cream

This is an outstanding flavor, appropriate especially for party desserts after Italian or Mexican foods. It leaves the palate with a clean, fresh taste.

Make Mint Ice Cream as directed. Then crush ¾ cup of chocolate mint candy, or use mint-flavored chocolate chips. Add to the Mint Ice Cream immediately after cranking, then complete the freezing as directed in Chapter II.

Peppermint Stick Ice Cream

This turns out a delicate pink color. Perfect for birthday parties!

> 1 **quart Half and Half**
> ½ **cup sugar**
> **A few grains of salt**
> 2 **teaspoons peppermint extract**
> ¾ **cup crushed peppermint stick candy**

Scald the Half and Half as directed in Chapter II. Add the sugar and salt. Cool, then add the peppermint extract. Chill and crank as directed in Chapter II.

Crush the peppermint stick candy by putting it into a clear plastic bag and hammering until the pieces are as small as you can get them. Add the crushed candy to the ice cream immediately after the cranking and then complete the freezing as directed in Chapter II. (If you get impatient and add the candy to the warm cream, the candy will dissolve and you'll miss out on the peppermint stick texture.)

Lemon Pie Ice Cream

Normally we avoid complicated recipes, but the appeal of lemon pie forced an attempt to produce a similar ice cream. The result, we think, justifies the additional work.

> 2 **cups sugar**
> 1 **cup water**
> ¾ **cup lemon juice (3 to 4 lemons)**
> 2 **cups Half and Half**
> 2 **egg yolks**

Boil the sugar and water together for about 5 minutes, stirring constantly to make a thick syrup. Squeeze the lemons to make ¾ cup of juice. Add to the hot sugar syrup and set aside.

Mix 1 cup of the Half and Half with the egg yolks and cook very slowly just below a boil, stirring, until you have created a thick lumpy mess sometimes called custard. This takes about 20 minutes of watching and stirring. Don't get impatient or you'll spoil it by allowing it to boil. Cool the custard mixture.

If you prefer a tarter taste, reduce the sugar to 1½ cups. If you prefer more of a custard taste, use 3 egg yolks.

Now combine the lemon syrup with the custard

mixture and the remaining cup of the Half and Half. Stirring will break up the lumps. (Any lumps remaining will disappear as you crank.) Chill, crank and freeze as directed in Chapter II.

Lemon Drop Ice Cream

Make Lemon Pie Ice Cream as directed. Crush ½ cup of lemon drop candies and stir them into the Lemon Pie Ice Cream immediately after cranking. Then complete the freezing as directed in Chapter II.

Orange Custard Ice Cream

2 cups sugar
1 cup water
3 cups fresh orange juice
  (6 to 7 oranges)
2 cups Half and Half
2 egg yolks

Boil the sugar and water for about 5 minutes, stirring constantly, to form a thick syrup. Squeeze the oranges to make 3 cups of juice. Add to the hot sugar syrup and set aside.

Mix one cup of the Half and Half with the egg yolks and cook very slowly without boiling until the whole thing turns lumpy—about 20 minutes. Stir regularly and keep the heat low to prevent burning or boiling. Cool, and then add the orange syrup and the remaining cup of Half and Half. Stir well and most of the lumps will vanish. Chill, crank and freeze as directed in Chapter II.

Butterscotch-Orange Custard Ice Cream

If you are really looking for something different, make the Orange Custard Ice Cream with brown sugar instead of white, thus creating a butterscotch-orange taste.

Pistachio Nut Ice Cream

This has always been one of our favorites. Making it, however, proves to be a bit of a chore—the nuts are a nuisance to shell and it takes a lot of them. But the true pistachio flavor bears little resemblance to the commercial. Note that your homemade ice cream will be colorless unless you color it green.

> ½ cup pistachio nuts
> 1 quart Half and Half
> ¾ cup sugar
>   A few grains of salt
>   A few drops of green food coloring
> 1 teaspoon almond extract (or 2 teaspoons pistachio nut extract)

Shell and mash the nuts. Add the mashed nuts to the Half and Half and slowly scald as directed in Chapter II. This brings out the nut flavor. Stir in the sugar and salt. After cooling, add a few drops of coloring and the almond or pistachio nut extract. Chill, crank and freeze as directed in Chapter II.

PISTACHIO NUT EXTRACT:

½ cup pistachio nuts
1 cup brandy

Shell and mash the nuts. Then combine the mashed nuts with the brandy. Place in a tightly covered jar and allow to stand for at least a month. Substitute 2 tablespoons of pistachio nut extract for the almond extract in the recipe for Pistachio Nut Ice Cream.

Pistachio Chocolate Chip Ice Cream

Make Pistachio Ice Cream as directed, and immediately after cranking stir in ½ cup chopped chocolate pieces or the same amount of chocolate chips. Finish freezing as directed in Chapter II.

Pistachio Fudge Nut Ice Cream

Make the Emperor's Fudge Sauce. Then make Pistachio Ice Cream. Transfer to a loaf pan after cranking and freeze as usual. When it is just short of hard, cut in the warm fudge sauce, following the directions for ribboning on page 31. Then freeze hard as directed in Chapter II.

Grandmother Sutherlin's
Indiana Farm Ice Cream

This old, old standard originally called for warm milk straight from the cow. The proportions of milk and cream depended on what was available at the time. The ingredients can be cooked together, but as Grandmother Sutherlin wrote: "We like it best not cooked; it will not be so smooth but still good."

> 3 **quarts milk**
> 1 **quart cream**
> 3 **cups sugar**
> 6 **eggs**

Follow Grandmother Sutherlin's method and stir all ingredients together until the sugar is dissolved and everything is well mixed. (Or you can follow our usual method and scald the milk and cream together as directed in Chapter II, then stir in the sugar until dissolved.) Remove from the heat and cool. Lightly beat the eggs to mix the whites and yolks, then slowly stir them into the lukewarm cream mixture. Put back over a low flame and cook very slowly without boiling until the mixture has thickened—about 20 minutes. Cool.

Chill, crank and freeze as directed in Chapter II.

Seasonal Specialties

One cannot eat one's cake and have it too.

—T. H. HUXLEY

These flavors can be considered "seasonal" either because they complement certain holidays (for example, eggnog and Christmas) or because the ingredients are seasonal (fresh peaches and summer). In either case the fact that you care enough to make your own ice cream will impress your guests. For the fresh fruit ice creams, note that they taste better after they've had time to "ripen" overnight, so do try to make them a day ahead of time.

All the recipes that follow make approximately one quart of ice cream, to serve four to six persons.

Apricot Ice Cream

2 cups fresh apricots
1½ cups sugar
1 pint Half and Half

Pit the apricots and cut them into small pieces. Then cook them with the sugar for about 10 minutes over medium heat. Stir regularly to prevent scorching. Remove from heat and stir in the Half and Half. Cool, then chill, crank and freeze as directed in Chapter II.

Blackberry Ice Cream

> 1 cup fresh blackberries
> 1 cup sugar
> 1 pint Half and Half

Crush the berries and add the sugar to them. You may vary the amount of sugar in accordance with your personal preferences and the sweetness of the berries. Either let the berries stand with sugar for 1 hour, or cook the berries and sugar over medium heat for 5 minutes, stirring constantly. Add the Half and Half, mix well and cool. Chill, crank and freeze as directed in Chapter II. This recipe also works beautifully with boysenberries or ollalie berries.

Ruth's Blueberry Ice Cream

> 1½ cups fresh blueberries (1 pint box)
> 1 cup sugar
> 1 pint Half and Half
> 1 teaspoon lemon juice
> 1 teaspoon pure vanilla extract

Mash the berries, mix with the sugar and let stand at room temperature for at least one hour. Run this mix through a blender and then simmer for about 20 minutes, stirring often. Cool, then stir in the Half and Half, lemon juice and vanilla extract. Chill, crank and freeze as directed in Chapter II.

Frozen Blueberry Ice Cream

If you must have a dish of blueberry ice cream in midwinter, make it with frozen blueberries. It won't quite equal fresh blueberry, but it will remind you that winter isn't forever.

> 1 10-ounce package of frozen blueberries
> 2 tablespoons sugar
> 1 pint Half and Half
> 1 teaspoon lemon juice
> 1 teaspoon pure vanilla extract

Thaw the berries, then put all the ingredients except the vanilla extract in the blender and blend until smooth. Simmer for 5 minutes, stirring often. Cool, then add the vanilla extract, and chill, crank and freeze as directed in Chapter II.

Fresh Raspberry Ice Cream

> 1 cup fresh raspberries
> 1 cup sugar
> 1 pint Half and Half
> 1 teaspoon lemon juice

Crush the berries and pour the sugar over them. The exact amount of sugar will vary with your personal preference and with the sweetness of the berries.

Let the fruit and sugar stand one hour at room temperature, then mix in the Half and Half and the lemon juice. Chill, crank and freeze as directed in Chapter II.

Frozen Raspberry Ice Cream

1 pint Half and Half
1 tablespoon sugar
1 10-ounce package frozen raspberries
A few grains of salt
2 teaspoons pure vanilla extract
1 teaspoon lemon juice

Scald the Half and Half as directed in Chapter II. Add the sugar and allow the mixture to cool. Mash the thawed berries and add them along with the salt, vanilla extract and lemon juice. Chill, crank and freeze as directed in Chapter II.

Strawberry Ice Cream

1 cup fresh strawberries
½ cup sugar
1 pint Half and Half
2 teaspoons pure vanilla extract
1 teaspoon lemon juice
A few grains of salt

Mash the berries and mix with the sugar. Let them stand at room temperature for about one hour, then mix with the remaining ingredients. Chill, crank and freeze as directed in Chapter II.

Peach Ice Cream

          2 cups fresh peaches
         ½ cup sugar
          1 pint Half and Half
         ½ teaspoon lemon juice
             A few grains of salt
          1 teaspoon pure vanilla extract

Peel the peaches and cut them into small pieces. Pour the sugar over them and let them stand at room temperature for about an hour. Now mix the Half and Half with one cup of the peaches and blend completely smooth in a blender. Then stir in the remaining cup of sugared peaches along with the rest of the ingredients. Chill, crank and freeze as directed in Chapter II.

Note: blending half of the peaches spreads the peach flavor and color, while the rest of the peach chunks add texture. Your peach ice cream will taste better the second day, as it takes a while for all the peach flavor to develop. So if you're planning a party, make it ahead.

Pumpkin Pie Ice Cream

If you like pumpkin pie, you'll really enjoy this ice cream—it tastes like frozen pumpkin pie. Simple and different!

    1 1-pound can of pumpkin
    ¾ cup brown sugar
    1 egg
    1 pint Half and Half
    ½ teaspoon salt
    1 teaspoon cinnamon
    ½ teaspoon ginger
    ¼ teaspoon cloves
      A sprinkle of nutmeg

All you do with this is mix all of the above ingredients together very carefully. Then chill, crank and freeze as directed in Chapter II.

Eggnog Ice Cream

It wasn't easy to get this recipe just right, but we believe you'll find our efforts worthwhile. This makes a festive Christmas season dessert.

    1 cup Half and Half
    4 eggs
    1 cup homogenized milk
    ½ cup sugar
    ½ teaspoon pure vanilla extract
      A generous sprinkling of nutmeg

Scald the Half and Half as directed in Chapter II. Cool. Beat the eggs thoroughly and stir in the milk, the scalded Half and Half, sugar, vanilla extract and nutmeg. Beat again, then chill, crank and freeze as directed in Chapter II.

For added appeal sprinkle nutmeg over each dish of eggnog ice cream at serving time.

viii

Hawaiian Ice Cream

*Every sunset which I witness inspires me with
the desire to go to a West as distant and
fair as that into which the sun goes down.*

—HENRY DAVID THOREAU

The flavors described in this chapter will bring a hint
of Hawaii to your home. Many ingredients, like
bananas and coconut, are available everywhere. And
thanks to speedy air transportation, other fresh
Hawaiian fruits can generally be found in mainland
markets.

All the recipes that follow make approximately
one quart of ice cream, to serve four to six persons.

Banana Ice Cream

The flavor is great!

1 quart Half and Half
¾ cup sugar
4 ripe bananas
1¼ tablespoons lemon juice

Scald the Half and Half as directed in Chapter II.
Stir in the sugar and let cool. Choose very ripe
bananas and peel and mash them. Put the mashed
bananas and about one cup of the scalded Half and
Half in a blender and purée. Then stir in the remaining Half and Half and the lemon juice. Chill,
crank and freeze as directed in Chapter II.

Banana Macadamia Nut Ice Cream

This flavor combines two of Hawaii's tastiest
products. Canned macadamia nuts can be found
throughout the United States. In fact they cost less in
Arcadia, California, than in Honolulu. Broken
macadamia nuts are cheaper, and save you the trouble
of chopping. You'll find this a popular party dessert.

Make Banana Ice Cream as directed, and, immediately after cranking, stir in ½ cup chopped macadamia nuts. Finish freezing as directed in Chapter II.

Banana Fudge Ribbon Ice Cream

Make Emperor's Fudge Sauce. Then make Banana
Ice Cream, put it into a loaf pan after cranking and
freeze as usual. When it is just short of hard, cut in
the warm fudge sauce, following the directions for
ribboning on page 31. Then freeze hard as directed
in Chapter II.

Coconut Ice Cream

The fresh coconut lends a superior flavor to this ice cream.

    1 **cup chopped fresh coconut (1 medium coconut)**
    1 **quart Half and Half**
    ¾ **cup sugar**

Open the coconut by holding it on a hard surface and striking it smartly with a hammer. Scoop out the meat and chop it into very small pieces. Or put the coconut meat into a plastic bag and smash it with a mallet or hammer. This will yield about 1 cup.

Scald the Half and Half as directed in Chapter II. Then add the sugar and ½ cup of the chopped coconut and put in the blender at high speed until completely blended. Stir in the remaining ½ cup of coconut—the unblended coconut pieces will lend a pleasing texture. Chill, crank and freeze as directed in Chapter II.

Ginger Ice Cream

Fresh ginger root can be found in most large supermarkets.

    1 **teaspoon fresh ginger**
    1 **quart Half and Half**
    ¾ **cup sugar**

First, peel your piece of fresh ginger. Then put it in a saucepan with the Half and Half and scald as directed in Chapter II. The ginger flavor will now be transferred to the cream. Remove the ginger and add the sugar. (If you are especially fond of it, you can blend the piece of ginger into the Half and Half for added strength.) Cool, then chill, crank and freeze as directed in Chapter II.

Macadamia Nut Ice Cream

½ cup chopped macadamia nuts
1 quart Half and Half
¾ cup sugar
   A few grains of salt
1 teaspoon almond extract (or 2 tablespoons
   macadamia nut extract)

Chop the macadamia nuts, add them to the Half and Half and scald as directed in Chapter II. As with the ginger, this will bring out the nut flavor. Stir in the sugar and salt, and cool. Then add the almond extract. (Or if you plan ahead, you can make a sort of macadamia nut extract which adds still more flavor.) Chill, crank and freeze as directed in Chapter II.

MACADAMIA NUT EXTRACT :

½ cup macadamia nuts
1 cup brandy

Chop and mash the nuts. Then put them into a small bottle with one cup of brandy. Seal tightly and store in a cool place for at least a month (better yet, two to three months). The brandy will extract the nut flavor. Substitute 2 tablespoons of macadamia nut extract for the almond extract in the above recipe.

Macadamia Chocolate Chip Ice Cream

Make Macadamia Nut Ice Cream as directed, and immediately after cranking stir in ½ cup of chopped chocolate pieces or the same amount of chocolate chips, and finish freezing as directed in Chapter II.

Macadamia Fudge Ribbon Ice Cream

Make Emperor's Fudge Sauce. Then make Macadamia Ice Cream, put it into a loaf pan after cranking, and freeze as usual. When it is just short of hard, cut in the warm fudge sauce, following the directions for ribboning on page 31. Then freeze hard.

Mango Ice Cream

You probably won't find this flavor at your supermarket unless you live in Hawaii. So, if you're searching for something different, this may be it. Mangoes do appear in mainland stores in the late spring. Let the fruit ripen completely, like peaches. The ice cream will turn out an attractive orange color.

2 mangoes
1 pint Half and Half
¾ cup sugar
1 teaspoon lemon juice
4 drops almond extract
A few grains of salt

Peel the mangoes and slice them informally. You'll find them quite juicy. Put the mango slices and the Half and Half in a blender and thoroughly amalgamate. This will yield approximately 3½ cups of thin purée.

Stir in the sugar, lemon juice, almond extract and salt. (Almond extract helps bring out the mango flavor.) Chill, crank and freeze as directed in Chapter II.

A NOTE ON PINEAPPLE ICE CREAM

Making pineapple ice cream proved educational. We had thought that fresh pineapple would give the truest taste. Unfortunately, fifteen minutes after we had combined fresh pineapple with the Half and Half, the mix had a curdled appearance. One taste was more than enough: this bitterness would never be cured by adding sugar! Only then did we recall that fresh pineapple contains an enzyme, bromelin, which breaks down proteins. What happens is that the enzyme partially digests the cream. (This same enzyme will attack gelatins, which is why one can't use fresh pineapple in Jell-O salads.) The solution is to heat the pineapple, which inactivates the enzyme.

The work of cooking pineapple may lead you to use canned pineapple instead, but canned pineapple doesn't usually taste much like the fresh. However, a new type of canned pineapple has recently been developed—it is water-packed without added sugar, and tastes just like fresh fruit. Pineapple Ice Cream II is made with this.

Pineapple Ice Cream I

> 1 pint Half and Half
> ⅓ cup sugar
> 1 cup fresh pineapple
> A few grains of salt

First scald the Half and Half as directed in Chapter II. Add the sugar and let cool.

Cut the fresh pineapple into small chunks and mash them to yield both crushed fruit and juice. (The juice will spread the fruit flavor and color the ice cream, while the pineapple chunks add texture as well.) Put the crushed pineapple and its juice and the salt into a saucepan over *very* low heat (no more than 150 degrees) for 30 minutes. (Heating at higher temperature wil change the flavor.)

Mix the cooked pineapple with the scalded Half and Half. Chill, crank and freeze as directed in Chapter II.

Pineapple Ice Cream II

We heartily recommend this water-packed "no sugar added" canned pineapple for your ice cream.

> 1 pint Half and Half
> ¼ cup sugar
> 1 cup canned water-packed crushed
>   pineapple (without added sugar)
> A few grains of salt

Scald the Half and Half as directed in Chapter II. Add the sugar and let cool. Mix in the crushed water-packed pineapple with its liquid and the salt, and chill, crank and freeze as directed in Chapter II.

Papaya Ice Cream

Papayas are yellow when ripe. Like pineapple, they also contain an enzyme which breaks down the protein in milk or cream, thus producing a slightly bitter taste. As with pineapple, papaya must be heated to inactivate the enzyme.

> 1 large papaya
> 1 pint Half and Half
> ½ cup sugar
> 2 tablespoons lemon juice
> ¼ cup orange juice

Scoop the papaya out of its skin and scrape out the seeds. Finely chop the papaya fruit. (This will yield about a cupful.) Put the chopped papaya into a saucepan over *very* low heat (no more than 150 degrees), stirring occasionally, for about 30 minutes.

Scald the Half and Half as directed in Chapter II, then add the sugar. Cool, then stir in the cooked chopped papaya along with the lemon juice and orange juice. Chill, crank and freeze as directed in Chapter II.

ix

Sure-Fire
Sherbets

One swallow makes not a spring,
nor one woodcock a winter.

—JOHN RAY

Their fresh fruit flavor combined with lightness makes sherbets ideal desserts. Some have a tart taste that makes them suitable for side dishes during fancy dinners.

Technically, sherbets must contain milk products, but sherbets have a lower concentration of fat and higher acidity and sugar content than ice cream. We use homogenized milk in our sherbets and have found that even skim milk works well—skim milk would be good for dieters, or people on low cholesterol intake.

As far as we're concerned, it is a waste of time to mess around with gelatin, eggs or boiling water for sherbet. All you really need is fruit or fruit juice, milk and sugar. Chilling, cranking and freezing are the same as for ice cream.

All the recipes that follow make approximately one quart of sherbet, to serve four to six persons.

Lemon Sherbet

This flavor is much more delicate than that of artificially flavored commercial varieties. And unless you color it, this lemon sherbet turns out almost white.

> 1 cup fresh lemon juice (3 to 4 lemons)
> ¾ cup sugar
> 1 pint milk
> A few drops of yellow artificial food coloring (optional)

Squeeze the lemons to make 1 cup of juice. Add the sugar and stir well until dissolved. Then combine with the milk, add a few drops of yellow food coloring if you like, and chill, crank and freeze as directed in Chapter II.

Lime Sherbet

In popularity lime sherbet ranks just ahead of lemon. As with lemon, homemade lime sherbet has a lighter, purer taste than store-bought. Again, we suggest artificial food coloring to lend a healthy green color. If you really are a "limey," you can strengthen the flavor by adding one tablespoon more juice to make it more tart. In any case, with chilling and aging, the lime flavor becomes more pronounced.

½ cup lime juice (about 4 limes)
½ cup sugar
    A few grains of salt
1 pint milk
    A few drops of green artificial food coloring
    (optional)

Squeeze the limes to make ½ cup of juice. Stir in the sugar and salt until dissolved. Combine with the milk, add a few drops of green artificial food coloring if you wish, and chill, crank and freeze as directed in Chapter II.

Orange Sherbet I

This old standby leads all other sherbets in popularity. We have found that fresh orange juice makes the best orange sherbet. The natural color is a pale orange, so you may want to add coloring.

1½ to 2 cups fresh orange juice (4 to 6 oranges)
¼ cup lemon juice (1 lemon)
¾ cup sugar
    A few grains of salt
1 pint milk
    A few drops of orange artificial food coloring
    (optional)

Squeeze the oranges to make 1½ or 2 cups of juice (2 cups of juice gives a stronger flavor). Squeeze the lemon to make ¼ cup of juice and add to the orange juice. Add the sugar and salt; stir well to dissolve. Then combine with the milk, add a few drops of artificial food coloring if you like, and chill, crank and freeze as directed in Chapter II.

Orange Sherbet II

If you are in a rush, this will do.

1½ cups prepared frozen orange juice
1 tablespoon frozen orange juice concentrate
1 cup sugar
   A few grains of salt
1 pint milk

Mix these ingredients, stirring well to dissolve the sugar, and chill, crank and freeze as directed in Chapter II.

Orange-Chocolate Sherbet

Do you like the combination of chocolate and orange? Ruth Dueker never could get used to her boys eating orange sherbet with chocolate sauce. Nevertheless, this is an old, tried combination—in fact Grandmother Learned liked to serve orange-chocolate candy. This sherbet looks like chocolate ice cream, but ah, the taste!

2 squares (2 ounces) unsweetened chocolate
1 quart milk
1 cup sugar
   A few grains of salt
1½ cups fresh orange juice

Put the chocolate into the top of a double boiler over boiling water until melted, stirring occasionally.

When melted, stir in the milk and scald as directed on page 19. Strain to remove the lumps; add the sugar and salt. Cool. Stir in the orange juice. Chill, crank and freeze as directed in Chapter II.

Tangerine Sherbet

Tangerines aren't so easy to squeeze as oranges since they tend to fall apart, but stick with it: you'll like this sherbet. Note that an average tangerine yields about ½ cup juice.

> **2 cups fresh tangerine juice (4 to 5 tangerines)**
> **1 cup sugar**
> **1 cup milk**

Squeeze the tangerines to make 2 cups of juice. Stir in the sugar until dissolved. Add the milk, then chill, crank and freeze as directed in Chapter II. (Note: if you want a tarter sherbet, reduce the sugar to ¾ cup.)

Raspberry Sherbet I

> **2 cups raspberries**
> **2 cups sugar**
> **1 pint milk**
> **1 tablespoon lemon juice**

Mash the raspberries and put into a small saucepan with the sugar. Cook over medium-low heat at a slow boil for 10 minutes. Put into a blender, add the milk and blend at high speed until smooth. Strain to remove seeds and pulp. Cool, then stir in the lemon juice. Chill, crank and freeze as directed in Chapter II.

Raspberry Sherbet II

    1 10-ounce package frozen raspberries
    1 tablespoon sugar
    ¾ cup milk
    ½ teaspoon lemon juice

Thaw the berries and then put them into a blender at high speed until liquefied. Strain the resulting juice to remove the seeds. This will give you about 1 cup of juice. Stir in the sugar until dissolved, then stir in the milk and lemon juice. Chill, crank and freeze as directed in Chapter II.

Strawberry Sherbet

    2 cups strawberries
    2 cups sugar
    1 pint milk
    1 tablespoon lemon juice

Wash strawberries gently (put them into a bowl of cold water to loosen sand, lift out and pat dry with paper towels). Hull them, and then mash them with a fork. Put the mashed strawberries into a small saucepan with the sugar over a medium-low flame and cook at a slow boil for 10 minutes. Then put into a blender with the milk, and blend at high speed until smooth.

Strain to remove seeds and any pulp. Cool. Add lemon juice at the last moment, then chill, crank and freeze as directed in Chapter II.

Blueberry Sherbet

>   2 cups blueberries
> 1½ cups sugar
>   1 pint milk
>   1 tablespoon lemon juice

Wash the berries, put into a saucepan with the sugar and cook over a medium-low flame for about 10 minutes at a slow boil. Put into a blender with the milk and blend at high speed until smooth. Then strain, and discard the pulp. Stir in the lemon juice. Chill, crank and freeze as directed in Chapter II.

Boysenberry Sherbet

This works nicely with blackberries and ollalie berries, too.

>   2 cups boysenberries
> 1½ cups sugar (or more, to taste)
>   1 pint milk

Crush the berries and add the sugar. Put into a saucepan over a medium-low flame and cook at a low boil for about 10 minutes. Put into a blender with the milk and blend thoroughly at high speed until smooth. Strain and discard seeds and pulp. Chill, crank and freeze as directed in Chapter II.

Cranberry Sherbet

Create this tasty and unusual seasonal sherbet with fresh cranberries. A scoop of it in a paper muffin container will dress up a holiday turkey dinner.

1 pound fresh cranberries
4 cups boiling water
½ to 1 cup sugar
½ cup milk
1 teaspoon lemon juice
1 teaspoon orange juice

Cook the berries in the water until they pop open and become soft (10 to 15 minutes). Strain, and discard the skins. This will give you about 3 cups of cranberry juice. Add the sugar. (The amount of sugar you add depends on how tart you want the sherbet to be. One-half cup will give a taste about equal to that of cranberry sauce.) Mix the cooked, sweetened cranberry juice into the milk. Stir in the lemon and orange juices. Cool, then chill, crank and freeze as directed in Chapter II.

Grape Sherbet

This makes a colorful sherbet. Kids love it.

3 cups unsweetened bottled
grape juice
1 cup sugar
1 pint milk
2 tablespoons lemon juice

Mix all the ingredients, stirring well to dissolve the sugar, and chill, crank and freeze as directed in Chapter II.

Apricot Sherbet

During the summer, fresh apricots provide the basic ingredient for a fine sherbet.

> **2 cups apricots**
> **2 cups sugar**
> **1 pint milk**

Pit the apricots and put them into a saucepan with the sugar. Cook them over a medium-low flame at a low boil for about 10 minutes. Put into a blender with the milk, and blend at high speed to a smooth purée. Chill, crank and freeze as directed in Chapter II.

Apricot Nectar Sherbet

If you develop a craving for apricot sherbet in the middle of winter, try this recipe using canned apricot nectar:

> **2 cups canned apricot nectar**
> **2 tablespoons sugar**
> **1 cup milk**

Combine the ingredients, mix well, and chill, crank and freeze as directed in Chapter II.

Jamie's Watermelon Sherbet

A friend of ours from Kansas told us to try this one. The only drawback is that it doesn't keep well, so eat it within three days.

> 5 cups chopped watermelon
> (about 2 pounds watermelon)
> ½ cup sugar
> ½ cup milk
> ½ teaspoon lemon juice

Chill the watermelon, then cut off the rind and discard. Chop up the fruit to make 5 cups (or scoop out 5 cups of watermelon balls).

Put the chopped watermelon into a blender and blend at low speed until liquefied. You should have about 2 cups of watermelon juice. Strain the juice to remove any seed fragments. Stir in the sugar until dissolved, then add the milk and lemon juice. Chill, crank and freeze as directed in Chapter II.

Pineapple Sherbet I

In this sherbet you use the juice of fresh pineapple. As described on page 80, this must be cooked to inactivate the enzyme bromelin or it will sour the sherbet.

> 4 cups chopped fresh pineapple
> (1 or 2 pineapples)
> 1 cup water
> 6 tablespoons sugar
> 1 cup milk

Cut the pineapple lengthwise and cut out the fruit from the rind. (Work carefully to keep the rinds intact, and they will make unusual serving bowls for the sherbet.) Chop up the fruit, being sure to discard the central hard core. (You will need 1 or 2 pineapples to give 4 cups of chopped pineapple.) Put the chopped pineapple in a blender with 1 cup of water, blend at high speed to liquefy, then let stand for an hour or longer. Strain to remove the pulp, and you'll get about 2 cups of clear pineapple juice.

Put the pineapple into a saucepan over *very* low heat (no higher than 150 degrees) for 30 minutes. Stir in the sugar until dissolved, add the milk, then chill, crank and freeze as directed in Chapter II.

Pineapple Sherbet II

Use water-packed canned pineapple *without sugar—* this makes the finest sherbet. It also saves the work of cutting up a fresh pineapple, and it needs no cooking.

> 4 cups water-packed pineapple
>   without added sugar
>   (2 16-ounce cans)
> 1 cup water
> ¼ cup sugar
> 1 cup milk

Put the crushed pineapple into a blender with 1 additional cup of water, blend at high speed to liquefy, and strain. This should give you 2 cups of juice. Stir in the sugar until dissolved, and add the milk. Chill, crank and freeze as directed in Chapter II.

Pineapple Sherbet III

The simplest way to make pineapple sherbet is with canned pineapple juice—no blending, no straining, no cooking.

 2 cups canned unsweetened
 pineapple juice
 ¼ cup sugar
 1 cup milk

Mix the ingredients, stirring to dissolve the sugar. Chill, crank and freeze as directed in Chapter II.

Guava Sherbet

Frozen guava juice makes this delicious Hawaiian sherbet possible everywhere. The juice is presweetened and artificially colored, so the sherbet will be the color of the real guava fruit. Ideal for a luau!

 1 6-ounce can frozen guava
 concentrate
 2 tablespoons sugar
 1 cup milk
 A few grains of salt
 1 tablespoon lemon juice

Stir all ingredients together. (Use the guava juice as it comes from the can; do not mix with water.) Chill, crank and freeze as directed in Chapter II.

Passion Fruit Sherbet

Like guava, passion fruit sherbet can be made with
frozen concentrated passion fruit juice. This makes a
nice light dessert.

> 1 6-ounce can frozen passion
>   fruit juice concentrate
> ¼ cup sugar
> 1 cup milk
>   A few grains of salt
> 1 tablespoon lemon juice

Mix all ingredients. (Do not dilute the concentrated
passion fruit juice. Use it straight from the can.)
Make sure the sugar is dissolved, then chill, crank
and freeze as directed in Chapter II.

Passion Fruit-Orange Sherbet

Personally, we prefer this combination to pure
passion fruit sherbet.

> ¾ cup fresh orange juice
>   (2 or 3 oranges)
> 3 ounces frozen passion fruit
>   juice concentrate
> 2 tablespoons lemon juice
> 6 tablespoons sugar
>   A few grains of salt
> 1 cup milk

Squeeze the oranges to make ¾ cup juice. Add the
concentrated passion fruit juice straight from the can

(do not dilute) and the lemon juice. Stir in the sugar and salt until dissolved. Mix with the milk, then chill, crank and freeze as directed in Chapter II.

Mango Sherbet

This sherbet has no equal as far as we are concerned. Mangoes don't need cooking or straining, and they make delicious sherbets. Mainland markets often have mangoes in late spring. Choose fully ripe ones—these are reddish with the consistency of a peach.

3 mangoes
2 cups sugar
1 pint milk
2 teaspoons lemon juice

Peel, pit and cut the mangoes into large chunks. Put them into a blender with the rest of the ingredients and blend at high speed until smooth. Chill, crank and freeze as directed in Chapter II.

Papaya Sherbet

You should be able to find fresh papaya in most large markets. As described on page 82, papaya needs cooking to deactivate the enzyme which would otherwise cause the sherbet to be bitter.

2 papayas
1 pint milk
1 cup sugar
¼ cup lemon juice

Cut the papayas in half like a melon. Remove the seeds and scoop out the fruit. Put the fruit into a blender and blend at high speed until liquefied. Then put the papaya liquid into a saucepan over very low heat (no more than 150 degrees), stirring occasionally, for about 30 minutes. Stir in the milk and sugar and cool. When cool, add the lemon juice. Chill, then crank and freeze as directed in Chapter II.

Jam Sherbets

In the spirit of frozen adventure we tried making sherbets from some of our homemade jams. The results were truly encouraging.

As a general method, mix equal quantities of jam and milk, put into a blender and blend well. Then chill, crank and freeze the mix as directed in Chapter II. Nothing could be simpler. Just be sure to use good quality jam.

Ices

I love to call a spade a spade.

—JONATHAN SWIFT

Historically, ices were the first of the frozen desserts. As might be expected, they have a more crystalline texture than ice cream. Their clean, fresh taste makes them ideal for desserts following heavy meals. They can also be served as side dishes—sometimes called sorbets—with the main course of a formal dinner. Ices are a welcome treat for people on milk-free or low-fat diets.

HOW TO MAKE ICES

The mixture: Ices contain only sugar and water and fruit juice. As a rule, the sugar and water are boiled before fruit juice is added. If sweetened, canned or concentrated fruit juice is used, no boiling is needed.

You can experiment with any frozen juice. Some will require additional sugar, but you will learn how much to add with a little practice.

The freezing: You don't need an ice cream freezer to make ices—you can freeze them in the freezer compartment of your refrigerator. After mixing the ingredients as directed in the recipes, pour the liquid into a shallow pan and place it in the freezer. Ice trays (with the dividers removed) also work nicely. A standard ice tray holds one pint without danger of overflowing.

Freeze until the ice is almost solid. Depending on your freezer, this will take from one to three hours. Stir the mix once or twice during freezing to distribute the quickly frozen portions along the sides into the middle.

When the ice is almost solid, transfer it to the mixing bowl. Using a sturdy fork, break the ice into small pieces. Then use an electric mixer at low speed to beat the ice into a mushy state. Transfer the mushy ice back to its shallow pan or ice tray, put it back in the freezer and refreeze to the hardness you prefer. (Beating the semifrozen ice breaks down the large ice crystals so that your dessert will not look like an ice cube—ice cubes are difficult to handle delicately with a spoon, and they aren't very chewable!)

When made in this way, ices will have a pleasing texture. They can be served semihard or completely frozen.

Unless otherwise noted, these recipes make approximately one pint of ices, to serve two to four persons.

Lemon Ice

6   tablespoons sugar
1   cup water
½   cup fresh lemon juice
    (1 to 2 lemons)

Boil the sugar and water for 5 minutes. Cool.
Squeeze the lemons to make ½ cup of juice and stir
into the cooled sugar water. Pour into a shallow pan
or ice tray and freeze as directed on page 104.

Lime Ice

6   tablespoons sugar
1   cup water
½   cup fresh lime juice
    (1 to 2 limes)

Boil the sugar and water for 5 minutes. Cool.
Squeeze the limes to make ½ cup of juice and stir
into the cooled sugar water. Pour into a shallow pan or
ice tray and freeze as directed on page 104.

Orange Ice I

¼   cup sugar
1   cup water
2   cups fresh orange juice
    (3 to 4 oranges)

Boil the sugar and water for 5 minutes. Cool. Squeeze the oranges to make 2 cups of juice and stir into the cooled sugar water. Pour into a shallow pan or tray and freeze as directed on page 104.

Orange Ice II

2 tablespoons sugar
¼ cup water
1⅓ cups frozen orange juice

Boil the sugar and water for 5 minutes. Cool. Stir in the frozen orange juice, pour into a shallow pan or ice tray and freeze as directed on page 104.

Tangerine Ice

¼ cup sugar
1 cup water
1⅓ cups fresh tangerine juice
(4 tangerines)

Boil the sugar and water for 5 minutes. Cool. Squeeze the tangerines to make 1⅓ cups juice and stir into the cooled sugar water. Pour into a shallow pan or ice tray and freeze as directed on page 104.

Grapefruit Ice

1 tablespoon sugar
1 cup water
1 cup fresh grapefruit juice
(2 grapefruits)

Boil the sugar and water for 5 minutes. Cool.
Squeeze the grapefruit to make 1 cup juice and stir
into the cooled sugar water. Pour into a shallow pan
or ice tray and freeze as directed on page 104. If you
prefer a less tart taste, add more sugar.

Grape Ice

> ½ cup sugar
> 1 cup water
> 1 cup bottled unsweetened
>   grape juice

Boil the sugar and water for 5 minutes. Cool.
Stir in the grape juice, pour into a shallow pan or ice
tray and freeze as directed on page 104.

Apricot Nectar Ice

> 2 tablespoons sugar
> 1 cup water
> 2 cups canned apricot nectar

Boil the sugar and water for 5 minutes. Cool. Stir in
the apricot nectar, pour into a shallow pan or ice tray
and freeze as directed on page 104.

Pineapple Ice

> ¼ cup sugar
> 1 cup water
> 2 cups unsweetened canned
>   pineapple juice

Boil the sugar and water for 5 minutes. Cool. Stir in the pineapple juice, pour into a shallow pan or ice tray and freeze as directed on page 104.

Guava Ice

1 can frozen guava nectar
concentrate
3 cans water

Mix the guava nectar concentrate and the water as though making guava juice for drinking. Pour into a shallow pan or two ice trays and freeze as directed on page 104. This makes approximately one quart, to serve four to six persons.

Passion Fruit Ice

1 can frozen passion fruit
juice concentrate
2½ cans water

Mix the passion fruit juice concentrate and the water. Pour into a shallow pan or two ice trays and freeze as directed on page 104. This makes a little less than one quart, to serve four to six persons.

xi

The Ice Cream Bar

All work and no play makes Jack a dull boy.

—JAMES HOWELL

All of the flavors in this chapter mix liquors with ice cream for "adult" desserts. Do not try to increase the amounts of liquor given, because this retards freezing; also, do not heat any mix containing alcohol, because the flavor will be altered.

Unless otherwise noted, these recipes make approximately one quart of ice cream, to serve four to six persons.

Cherries Jubilee Ice Cream I

This tastes wonderful—but the color turns out a grayish purple, so you may want to use food coloring.

1 pint Half and Half
¼ cup sugar
½ cup canned pitted sweet cherries
½ cup syrup from same can
1 tablespoon lemon juice
2 tablespoons brandy
A few drops of red artificial food coloring (optional)

Scald the Half and Half as directed on page 19, then stir in the sugar and cool. Crush the cherries and stir them into the cooled Half and Half, together with the rest of the ingredients. Chill, crank and freeze as directed in Chapter II.

Cherries Jubilee Ice Cream II

This comes out white with flecks of cherries. How festive!

1 pint Half and Half
6 tablespoons sugar
2 teaspoons pure vanilla extract
2 tablespoons brandy
2 cups halved maraschino cherries, drained

Scald the Half and Half as directed on page 19, then stir in the sugar and cool. Add the vanilla extract. Chill and crank as directed in Chapter II. Immediately after cranking, stir in the brandy and the drained maraschino cherries. Finish freezing as directed in Chapter II.

Eggnog Ice Cream

If you prefer your eggnog spiked, you'll like this.

   1 **cup milk**
   1 **cup Half and Half**
  ½ **cup sugar**
   4 **eggs**
  ½ **teaspoon pure vanilla extract**
  ¼ **teaspoon nutmeg**
   1 **or 2 tablespoons rum or brandy,**
     to taste

Mix the milk and Half and Half and scald as directed in Chapter II. Stir in the sugar until dissolved. Cool. Beat the eggs until light and foamy and stir in the vanilla extract, nutmeg and 1 or 2 tablespoons of rum or brandy. Stir in the cooled milk and Half and Half, then chill, crank and freeze as directed in Chapter II.

Crème de Cacao Ice Cream

Aunt Mary suggested this popular flavor. All you really have to do is add crème de cacao to your homemade vanilla ice cream. The color will be a light tan.

   1 **quart Half and Half**
  ¾ **cup sugar**
     A few grains of salt
 1½ **tablespoons pure vanilla extract**
  ¼ **cup crème de cacao**

Scald the Half and Half as directed in Chapter II. Stir in the sugar and salt. Cool. Add the vanilla extract and the crème de cacao, and chill, crank and freeze as directed in Chapter II.

Jamaican Chocolate Ice Cream

This chocolate variation is always a crowd pleaser— try it at your next party.

> 2 squares (2 ounces) unsweetened chocolate
> 1 quart Half and Half
> 1 cup sugar
> A few grains of salt
> 2 teaspoons pure vanilla extract
> 6 tablespoons Tía Maria (chocolate liqueur)

Put the chocolate into the top of a double boiler over boiling water, stirring occasionally, until melted. Slowly stir in a little of the Half and Half to make a paste. Then slowly stir in the remaining Half and Half and scald as directed in Chapter II. Stir, remove from heat, and strain to eliminate any lumps. Stir in the sugar and salt until dissolved. Cool. Finally, add the vanilla extract and the Tía Maria, and chill, crank and freeze as directed in Chapter II.

Chocolate Rum Raisin Ice Cream

This is one of our family's favorites.

> 2 squares (2 ounces) unsweetened chocolate
> 1 quart Half and Half
> 1 cup sugar
> A few grains of salt
> 2 teaspoons pure vanilla extract
> ¼ cup light rum
> ½ cup raisins

Put the chocolate into the top of a double boiler over boiling water, stirring occasionally until melted. Slowly stir in a little of the Half and Half to make a paste. Then slowly stir in the remaining Half and Half, and scald as directed in Chapter II. Stir well, remove from heat and strain to eliminate chocolate lumps. Stir in the sugar and salt until dissolved. Cool, then add the vanilla extract and rum. Chill and crank as directed in Chapter II. Immediately after cranking, mix the raisins into the ice cream and complete the freezing.

Irish Coffee Ice Cream

> 4 teaspoons freeze-dried coffee
> 1 quart Half and Half
> 1 cup sugar
> ¼ cup Irish (or other) whiskey
> Whipped cream

Stir the freeze-dried coffee into the Half and Half and scald as directed in Chapter II. Stir in the sugar until dissolved. Cool, then stir in the Irish (or other) whiskey. Chill, crank and freeze as directed in Chapter II. Serve topped with whipped cream.

Kahlúa Coffee Ice Cream

This flavor needs no words of praise—just taste it.

> 2 tablespoons instant coffee
> 1 quart Half and Half
> ¾ cup sugar
> A few grains of salt
> 2 teaspoons pure vanilla extract
> 4 tablespoons Kahlúa
> (coffee liqueur)

Stir the instant coffee into the Half and Half and scald as directed in Chapter II. Stir in the sugar and salt until dissolved. Cool, then stir in the vanilla extract and the Kahlúa. Chill, crank and freeze as directed in Chapter II.

Grasshopper Ice Cream

The crème de menthe flavor stands out over the crème de cacao and lends a pleasant light green hue to the ice cream.

> 1 quart Half and Half
> 4 tablespoons sugar
> A few grains of salt
> 2 tablespoons crème de cacao
> 6 tablespoons green crème de menthe
> ¼ teaspoon peppermint extract

Scald the Half and Half as directed in Chapter II. Stir in the sugar and salt until dissolved. Cool, then stir in the liqueurs and peppermint extract. (If you don't particularly like crème de menthe, reduce it to 3 tablespoons and increase the peppermint extract to ½ teaspoon.) Chill, crank and freeze as directed in Chapter II.

Crème de Menthe Mint Chip Ice Cream

The green crème de menthe also makes this a pleasant light green.

> 1 **quart Half and Half**
> ¼ **cup sugar**
> **A few grains of salt**
> ¼ **cup green crème de menthe**
> ½ **teaspoon peppermint extract**
> ¾ **cup chopped chocolate mint candy**

Scald the Half and Half as directed in Chapter II. Add the sugar and salt and chill. Stir in the crème de menthe and peppermint extract, and chill and crank as directed in Chapter II.

Chop up the chocolate mint candy to make ¾ cup. Immediately after cranking, stir in the chopped chocolate mint candy and complete the freezing.

Pink Champagne Sherbet

The remains of the bottle can entertain onlookers!

> 4 tablespoons extra-fine
> granulated sugar
> 3 cups milk
> 2 cups pink champagne

Stir the sugar into the milk until dissolved. Then mix in the pink champagne, pour into a shallow pan or two ice trays and freeze as directed on page 21.

Orange Curaçao Sherbet

Orange Curaçao makes homemade orange sherbet more special.

> 1½ cups fresh orange juice
> (3 to 4 oranges)
> 1 quart milk
> ¾ cup sugar
> 2 tablespoons orange Curaçao

Squeeze the oranges to make 1½ cups of juice. Then combine all the ingredients, making sure the sugar is dissolved. Pour into a shallow pan or two ice trays and freeze as directed on page 21.

Chocolate Orange Curaçao Sherbet

Orange Curaçao beautifully complements this combination of chocolate and orange. Make plenty or you'll find it gone before you get to sample it!

        2 squares (2 ounces) unsweetened
          chocolate
        1 quart milk
        ¾ cup sugar
          A few grains of salt
        1 cup fresh orange juice
          (2 to 3 oranges)
        2 tablespoons orange Curaçao

Put the chocolate into the top of a double boiler over boiling water, stirring occasionally until melted. Slowly stir in a little of the milk to make a paste. Then slowly stir in the rest of the milk and scald as directed in Chapter II. Stir, remove from heat and strain to eliminate any lumps. Stir in the sugar and salt until dissolved. Chill. At the last minute, squeeze the oranges to make 1 cup of juice, then stir in the orange juice and the orange Curaçao. Crank and freeze as directed in Chapter II.

Mai Tai Ice

When served as a drink, this tourist favorite is served over crushed ice. Why not freeze the whole thing as we do in the following recipe? You'll find bottled Mai Tai mix and pomegranate juice in well-equipped liquor stores and supermarkets.

> **6 ounces bottled Mai Tai mix**
> **1 teaspoon pomegranate juice**
> **3 ounces water**
> **3 ounces light rum**

Just stir the ingredients together, put into a shallow pan or ice tray and freeze as directed on page 21. It tastes good, too, when frozen just to a pink slush. This makes approximately one pint of sherbet, to serve two to four.

Ice Cream Sauces

Take that, miss; what's sauce for a goose
is sauce for a gander.

—JONATHAN SWIFT

These sauces combined with the ice cream you've been making will make superlative sundaes, parfaits, milk shakes, sodas, etcetera, etcetera.

All recipes make about one cup of sauce—enough for approximately one quart of ice cream, to serve four to six persons.

ABOUT CHOCOLATE SAUCES

You will probably be most frequently requested to make chocolate sauces. These can be served over ice cream, used in milk shakes, or poured into ice cream for ribboning.

When you make chocolate sauces you have to choose between those best for serving almost immediately and those best for storing. Sauces with the right consistency at the time you make them will harden when stored in the refrigerator. (They can, however, be heated slowly for melting.) Conversely, the chocolate sauce which keeps the best is a little too thin until it has been chilled.

Old Faithful Chocolate Sauce

This sauce looks thin while warm but it keeps well in the refrigerator, thickening as it chills.

> 2 squares (2 ounces) unsweetened chocolate
> ¾ cup water
> 1 cup sugar
> A few grains of salt
> 1 tablespoon butter

Put the chocolate and water in the top of a double boiler over boiling water, stirring until melted. Then add the sugar, salt and butter. Continue cooking slowly for about 15 minutes until the sauce is smooth.

Bittersweet Chocolate Sauce

This also keeps well.

> 2 squares (2 ounces) semisweet cooking chocolate
> ¾ cup water
> 1 tablespoon sugar
> A few grains of salt
> 1 tablespoon butter

Put the chocolate and water in the top of a double boiler over boiling water. Stir in the sugar, salt and butter and stir continually until the chocolate has completely melted and the sauce is creamy. Refrigerate for at least 2 hours before serving.

Kahlúa Chocolate Sauce

After any chocolate sauce is cooked, stir in 3 tablespoons of Kahlúa liqueur per cup of sauce.

Mexican Chocolate Sauce

Add ¾ teaspoon of ground cinnamon to any chocolate sauce as it cooks. This makes a different and delicious sauce.

Emperor's Fudge Sauce

This rich, thick sauce is ideal for sundaes and for ribboned ice cream. It will harden if refrigerated because of its thickness but can be warmed for serving. Personally, we like it best warm.

2 squares (2 ounces) semisweet cooking chocolate
½ cup Half and Half
1 cup sugar
A few grains of salt
2 tablespoons butter

Put the chocolate and Half and Half in the top of a double boiler over simmering water so it heats slowly. Add the sugar, salt and butter, stirring while cooking this into a smooth sauce—it takes some patience to melt the chocolate without overheating the Half and Half.

Emperor's Fudge Nut Sauce

Stir ½ cup of chopped walnuts into the Emperor's Fudge Sauce while still warm.

Quick Fudge Sauce

Great for when you are in a hurry!

> **1 package (6 ounces) semisweet chocolate chips**
> **½ stick (2 ounces) butter**

Put the chocolate with the butter in the top of a double boiler over simmering water. Heat slowly and stir diligently until the ingredients are well blended. Serve while still slightly warm.

Carolyn's Dutch Mocha Fudge Sauce

This delicious sauce requires no cooking if you have the coffee made. The coffee lends a good bittersweet taste.

¼ cup sugar
¾ cup unsweetened Dutch cocoa
¼ cup cold strong coffee
¼ teaspoon pure vanilla extract
¾ cup whipping cream

Mix the sugar and cocoa together. Slowly pour in the coffee and stir well until dissolved. Add the vanilla extract and cream. Beat slowly to make the sauce smooth and free of cocoa lumps.

This sauce can be chilled for a few hours; after a longer period it will harden. If you want a warm sauce, use hot coffee and heat the cream before mixing.

Mocha Sauce

Stir one tablespoon of instant coffee into any chocolate sauce as it cooks. This coffee-chocolate combination is always popular. This is best for sundaes. (For milk shakes and sodas, use June's Coffee Syrup, which follows.)

June's Coffee Syrup

This is a strongly flavored syrup, ideal for milk shakes and sodas. (For sundaes, use the Mocha Sauce above.)

1 cup sugar
1 cup water
1 2-ounce jar instant coffee

Put the sugar and water into a saucepan and bring to a boil. Cook for 10 minutes, stirring, and then slowly stir in the instant coffee. It takes only a minute to dissolve the coffee.

Coffee Syrup with Tía Maria

Make June's Coffee Syrup, and when it has cooled stir in 2 tablespoons of Tía Maria liqueur. This makes a very different taste in milk shakes and sodas.

Vanilla Sauce

1 cup water
1¼ cups sugar
1 tablespoon pure vanilla extract

Put the sugar and water into a small saucepan over a medium flame. Bring to a slow boil and continue boiling for 10 minutes, stirring continually. Cool, then stir in the vanilla extract.

Marshmallow Sauce

The ingredients do tend to separate upon standing, so serve at once.

2 cups marshmallows
¼ cup water
¾ cup sugar

Cut up the marshmallows with a scissors, then put into the top of a double boiler over boiling water, stirring until melted. Add the water and sugar and cook for 20 minutes, stirring well.

Butterscotch Sauce

This tends to separate when allowed to stand, so make it just before serving.

> 1 **cup brown sugar**
> 2 **tablespoons butter**
> ½ **cup milk**

Put the sugar and butter into a double boiler over simmering water and stir until melted. Slowly stir in the milk, and cook for 20 minutes. Stir often, and don't let it boil.

Easy Butterscotch Sauce

This will harden upon standing, so serve it warm.

> 1 **6-ounce package of**
>   **butterscotch chips**
> 6 **tablespoons water**

Put the butterscotch chips into a double boiler over simmering water, stirring until melted. Then stir in the water and cook 15 minutes, stirring often.

Caramel Syrup

This has the texture of simple sugar syrup. In these proportions, caramel syrup will be pourable even if refrigerated.

1 cup granulated sugar
1 cup boiling water

Put the sugar into a skillet over a low flame and slowly heat until it melts and caramelizes (turns brown). This will take 15 to 20 minutes. Stir it all the while. Now stir in the boiling water. (It must be boiling, or the sugar-syrup will form a hard ball, which ruins everything.) Cook the syrup 5 to 10 minutes longer, stirring constantly.

Peppermint Sauce

This makes a tasty and unusual sauce that keeps well. The color is nice, too.

½ cup red and white peppermint
   hard candy
¾ cup boiling water

First crush the peppermint candy: put it in a clear plastic bag and hammer it. (This will cut the melting time.) Then put it into the top of a double boiler over hot water, stirring until melted. Stir in the boiling water and cook 15 minutes, stirring well. (Adding boiling water keeps the melted candy from hardening again.)

If you want a thicker syrup, use only ⅔ cup of water—but use the sauce at once, while still warm, since it will get quite hard when cooled.

ABOUT CRUSHED FRUIT SAUCES

Fresh or frozen fruit can be used as a flavorful ice cream sauce. A few suggestions: pineapple, strawberries, peaches, blueberries, raspberries or nectarines.

In general we prefer to add sugar to fresh fruit, though a ripe pineapple really needs no additional sugar. Your personal preference will dictate the amount of sugar; a good starting point is one-half cup sugar to two cups of cut-up fruit.

Sprinkle the sugar over the fruit and mash it slightly to release the fruit juices. Allow to stand for an hour before serving, which will enhance the flavor.

If you use frozen fruit, serve before it has completely thawed. The syrup will supply the needed sweetening.

To serve, simply spoon the fruit with its juice over ice cream, or use it to make fruit parfaits as directed on page 136.

Melba Sauce

This recipe remains true to its famous originator, Auguste Escoffier. This sauce can make a fancy dessert out of a dish of vanilla or peach ice cream. But for the ultimate, see Peach Melba, page 147.

1 cup fresh raspberries
¼ cup currant jelly

Crush the raspberries and mix into the jelly. Put
into a saucepan over a medium flame, and heat to
boiling while stirring constantly. Then lower heat
and simmer for 10 minutes, stirring often.

Sutherlin Strawberry Sauce

1 pint fresh strawberries
2 tablespoons sugar (or to taste)
1 teaspoon cornstarch
1 teaspoon water

Gently wash the berries in cold water, then pat dry
with paper towels. Remove the hulls and discard.
Crush the berries and mix with the sugar. (The
amount of sugar will vary with the berries and your
taste buds.) Put into a small saucepan, slowly heat to
boiling, then lower to a simmer. Mix the cornstarch
and water to a paste and add to the simmering berries.
Continue to simmer, stirring, for about 10 minutes.
Cool before serving.

xiii

Fountain Favorites

Variety's the very spice of life.
—WILLIAM COWPER

Combine your own ice creams and sauces to make super desserts. Your homemade sundaes, parfaits and milk shakes will easily surpass anything available in an ice cream parlor.

SUNDAES

For small sundaes, one quart of ice cream will serve four to six. For elaborate sundaes with several scoops of ice cream, one quart of Ice Cream will serve three.

For dinner desserts: Stick to light sundaes with one flavor of ice cream and one type of topping. Crushed fresh fruit served over vanilla or fruit ice creams will complement any meal. Or just sprinkle shaved chocolate over vanilla ice cream.

For Special Treats Outside Meal Times:

1. Banana Splits made with Peach, Strawberry, and Pineapple Ice Creams. Top with crushed fresh peaches, strawberry and pineapple sauces.

2. Hawaiian Sundaes made with Pineapple, Macadamia Nut, Coffee and Banana Ice Creams. Any crushed fruit sauce is good. Or you may want to try chocolate sauce, whipped cream, nuts and a cherry!

3. Central Winner: Top vanilla ice cream with a chocolate sauce, Marshmallow Sauce and Spanish peanuts.

PARFAITS

Parfaits are layered sundaes served in tall glasses. Pour a thick layer of sauce into the glass and add a scoop of ice cream. Then put in more sauce and another scoop of ice cream. Top with sauce. For variety, you can use a different sauce for each layer. Parfaits can be made several hours before a party and stored in the freezer. They make an easy and pretty dessert for a party. One quart of ice cream will make eight parfaits.

Some suggestions:

1. Mexican Chocolate Parfait: Vanilla or Chocolate Ice Cream layered with Mexican Chocolate Sauce.

2. Pistachio Fudge Parfait: Pistachio Ice Cream layered with a fudge sauce.

3. Crème de Cacao Parfait: Crème de Cacao Ice Cream layered with Kahlúa Chocolate Sauce.

4. Mint Parfait: Mint Ice Cream layered with a chocolate sauce.

5. Melba Parfait: Peach Ice Cream layered with Melba Sauce.

6. Chocolate Demon Parfait: Chocolate Ice Cream layered with Fudge Nut Sauce.

COUPES

You make a coupe by layering ice cream or sherbet and sliced fresh fruit in tall, slim glasses. Suit the coupe to a season, or follow a regional theme, using, for example, Hawaiian fruits. One quart of ice cream or sherbet will make four coupes.

Some suggestions:

1. Slice fresh pineapple and Pineapple Ice Cream

2. Slice fresh mango and Mango Ice Cream

3. Slice fresh papaya and Orange Sherbet

4. Slice fresh peaches and Peach or Vanilla Ice Cream

5. Slice fresh strawberries and Strawberry Ice Cream or Lemon Ice

SODAS

Put two scoops of ice cream in a large, tall glass with ¼ cup sauce or syrup, and fill with soda water.

Stir well; top with more soda water when the fizz dies down. Serve with straws and a spoon. One quart of ice cream will make four sodas.

Some suggestions:

1. Chocolate soda made with Chocolate Ice Cream and a chocolate sauce.

2. Coffee soda made with Coffee Ice Cream and June's Coffee Syrup.

3. Chocolate-Peppermint soda made with Chocolate Ice Cream and Peppermint Sauce.

4. Strawberry Soda made with Vanilla Ice Cream and Sutherlin Strawberry Sauce.

MILK SHAKES AND MALTEDS

You can make delicious milk shakes right at home using a blender. To make thick shakes, combine three parts of ice cream to one part of milk and one part of syrup. If you prefer malteds, add a teaspoon of malted milk powder. One quart of ice cream will make four milk shakes or malteds.

Some suggestions:

1. Coffee milk shake made with Coffee Ice Cream and June's Coffee Syrup.

2. Peanut Butter milk shake made with ¾ cup Vanilla Ice Cream, ¼ cup peanut butter and ¼ cup milk.

3. Peach Melba milk shake made with Peach Ice Cream and Melba Sauce.

4. Mango milk shake made with Mango Ice Cream and milk.

5. Vanilla milk shake made with Vanilla Ice Cream, 1 tablespoon pure vanilla extract and milk.

6. Easy Chocolate milk shake—use Vanilla Ice Cream, a chocolate sauce and milk.

FREEZES

Freezes differ from milk shakes in that they do not have any sauce added—they're just ice cream or sherbet blended with milk. Sherbet freezes are especially good. A good proportion is ¾ cup of ice cream or sherbet to ¼ cup milk. One quart of ice cream or sherbet will make four freezes.

Mango Sherbet Freeze: blend ¾ cup Mango Sherbet with ¼ cup milk. (This is our all-time favorite.)

Make your own favorite using the same proportions.

xiv

Ice Cream Desserts

I am glad that my Adonis
hath a sweet tooth in his head.

—JOHN LYLY

Ice cream really needs no adornment to be an excellent dessert; however, for parties and special occasions something a little fancier may be indicated.

Hollowed-out fruit shells make attractive serving dishes for sherbets. A pineapple works well for pineapple sherbet, or you can form balls of sherbet and pile them in half a watermelon rind. Orange baskets for orange sherbet can be shaped by cutting an orange so as to leave a bridgelike handle attached to half of the orange peel. As you cut the fruit out of it, be careful not to pierce the peel.

MOLDED ICE CREAM

For the even more ambitious, molded ice creams make unusual and decorative desserts. The ice cream is frozen in the mold, which is removed before serving.

Selecting and preparing your mold: Gelatin salad molds or true ice cream molds may be used, and both types work well. Unfortunately, ice cream molds are difficult to find these days, although they are being made in France. They range from simple forms to elaborate miniatures of lambs and rabbits. The seams of ice cream molds are not fluid-tight, and so you must work quickly with them to prevent the ice cream from melting and running out between the two halves of the mold. You will find it helpful to cover the seams with plastic food wrap before putting in the ice cream. Gelatin molds are in one piece, so they have no leakage problem.

When you start making your ice cream, put the mold in the refrigerator freezer to chill. It will greatly ease the later task of unmolding if you spray the inside of the mold with PAM, a vegetable fat lubricant.

How to pack and freeze the mold: Make your ice cream and let it harden for about two hours to a semihard state, then transfer it to the chilled mold. (Obviously, completely hardened ice cream can't be put into a mold.) Pack the ice cream in firmly to ensure the most accurate reproduction of the mold's shape. Cover the exposed ice cream at the bottom of a gelatin mold with plastic wrap or aluminum foil and place the mold in your refrigerator's freezer.

Allow the ice cream to harden completely. This will take 18 to 24 hours.

How to unmold: Unmolding ice cream requires both practice and patience. The best way is to cover the mold with a hot towel that is wet but not dripping— dip the towel in very hot water, then wring out before applying. First remove the plastic wrap or foil covering the ice cream, then reverse the mold and set it onto a chilled serving dish. Place the hot towel around the mold for a few seconds. The heat will soften the surface just enough to let the ice cream slip out onto the dish. (Some suggest briefly dipping the molds in hot water. Don't do it: water will leak in and ruin the ice cream's surface. Even in leakproof gelatin molds, there will be sufficient melting to destroy the surface detail of the ice cream.)

If you're using a French ice cream mold, you can disassemble it from around the ice cream. Work carefully and quickly; the last side may require rubbing with the hot towel.

Return the unmolded ice cream to the freezer until you are ready to serve it. If the freezer stay is to exceed an hour, lightly cover the work of art with waxed paper to prevent frost formation.

To serve: Take the ice cream out of the freezer and let it stand for a few minutes at room temperature. Now quickly garnish the dish with such things as nuts and maraschino cherries, if you like. For the proper effect, bring your molded creation to the table and cut it there. A wide pastry server works better than a knife or spoon for cutting and serving.

It definitely takes a little effort to become an expert with molded ice creams. Start with a simple gelatin mold and practice until you can climax a fine dinner by bringing out a white ice cream lamb on a bed of shredded green coconut.

Molds vary in size from less than a quart to a half-gallon. Every quart serves four to six.

ICE CREAM AND
FRUIT DESSERTS

Cherries Jubilee

This is one of the best known and most dramatic of flamed desserts—your guests will surely be impressed.

1 **tablespoon sugar**
1 **8-ounce can of pitted sweet black cherries**
1 **recipe Vanilla Ice Cream**
½ **cup brandy**

In the kitchen, mix 1 tablespoon of sugar with the fruit and juice from the can of pitted sweet black cherries and put into a saucepan over moderate heat until piping hot but not boiling. Put the hot cherries and their juice into a bowl and bring to the table.

Put the homemade Vanilla Ice Cream into individual serving dishes and bring them to the table.

Slightly warm the brandy—the easiest way is to put the brandy into a ladle and hold it over a medium burner, or over a match flame, for a minute or two. Then bring it to the table in its ladle.

To serve, light a match, ignite the warmed brandy and pour it over the cherries, stirring until the flame has died down. Then spoon the cherry sauce over the ice cream, and serve at once.

Peach Melba

Auguste Escoffier created Peach Melba in 1894 to honor the great opera star. We suggest omitting the carved ice swan he served it in, but otherwise to remain true to the great chef. Note that you can prepare all the ingredients well in advance of party time.

> 4 **peaches**
> 1 **cup water**
> 1 **cup sugar**
> 1 **tablespoon pure vanilla extract**
> 1 **cup fresh raspberries**
>   **(frozen, if you must)**
> ¼ **cup currant jelly**
> 1 **pint Vanilla Ice Cream**

First prepare the peaches. Use fresh ones if possible or, off season, home-preserved ones. (Try not to use commercially canned or frozen peaches, as the flavor will not be right.) Peel the peaches by dropping them into boiling water for about 10 seconds. Then lift them out with a slotted spoon—the skins will now slip off easily. Cut the peaches in half and discard the pits.

Put the water and sugar into a saucepan and bring to the boil, then lower to a simmer. Put in the peach halves and simmer, covered, for 15 to 20 minutes. Remove from heat. When cool, add the vanilla extract, then chill. (If you are using peaches preserved in syrup, you need only stir the vanilla extract into the syrup. No cooking is required.)

To make the Melba Sauce: Crush the raspberries, then put them into a small saucepan with the currant jelly. Heat to the boiling point while stirring constantly, then simmer for 10 minutes. Chill. We do not strain this sauce as the raspberry seeds are not noticeable.

To serve: Put two peach halves in each dish, add a generous serving of Vanilla Ice Cream and top with the Melba Sauce. Or you may follow Escoffier and put the ice cream on the bottom.

Serves four.

Peaches Sutherlin

In 1970 a dessert fancier suggested that strawberries might go nicely with peaches and ice cream. Here is our original recipe for her. This is a fine winter dessert if you plan ahead by dry-freezing strawberries and peaches.

> 1 teaspoon cornstarch
> 1 teaspoon water
> 1 pint of strawberries (about 2 cups)
> 2 tablespoons sugar
> 1 tablespoon pure vanilla extract
> 4 fresh peaches: peeled, pitted, halved
> 1 pint Peach or Vanilla Ice Cream

First make a paste by mixing the teaspoonful of cornstarch with the teaspoonful of water.

Wash the strawberries and pat dry with paper towels. Then hull them and crush them in a saucepan. Add the sugar and bring to a boil. Reduce heat, add the cornstarch paste and simmer for 10 minutes while stirring continuously. Take off the fire. When cool, add the vanilla extract, then chill.

To serve: Place two peach halves in each dessert

bowl. Add a scoop of Peach or Vanilla Ice Cream, and top with the chilled strawberry sauce.

Serves four.

Poires Belle Hélène

> 1 recipe chocolate sauce
> 4 fresh ripe pears
> 1 cup sugar
> 1 cup water
> 1 tablespoon pure vanilla extract
> 1 pint Vanilla Ice Cream

First make your chocolate sauce (or defrost it if you've got some in the freezer).

Peel and halve the pears, and remove the cores. Put the water and sugar into a saucepan and bring to a boil, then lower to simmer. Put in the pear halves and simmer, covered, for 15 minutes, then remove from heat. When cool, add the vanilla extract, then chill.

To serve: Use flat dishes with a rim. Place a scoop of Vanilla Ice Cream in the center of each dish. Prop two pear halves up over the ice cream—pup-tent formation. Now pour the chocolate sauce over all.

Serves four.

ICE CREAM PIES

For something different, make an ice cream pie for a party dessert. It can be made several days in advance since the frozen crust won't get stale.

How to make ice cream pies: Freeze your ice cream in the usual fashion. Harden the ice cream for about two hours to a semihard state, and then spoon it into the *frozen* pie shell.

Put the pie back into the freezer and finish hardening. Cover it with waxed paper to prevent frost formation.

To serve: Take the pie out of the freezer and let it stand for 10 minutes at room temperature before serving. You may choose to decorate the pie with whipped cream or one of the ice cream sauces.

Pie crusts: Any kind of pie crust can be used to make ice cream pies. For your convenience, we'll give the recipes for four types. It's easiest to use one of the crumb types, since they don't require cooking.

Each pie crust recipe make a 9-inch pie shell. It takes about one pint of ice cream to fill each, and the 9-inch ice cream pie will serve six to eight.

Graham Cracker Pie Crust

20 single or 10 double graham crackers (to make 1⅔ to 1¾ cups of fine crumbs)
6 tablespoons butter
¼ cup sugar

Crush or blend the crackers into fine crumbs to yield 1⅔ to 1¾ cups. An easy way is to put the crackers into a plastic food bag and roll with a rolling pin. Put the butter into a small saucepan over very low heat until just melted. (Do not cook.) Mix the crumbs, sugar and melted butter. Pour into a lightly buttered 9-inch pie pan.

Pat the crust evenly over the pan—your own clean fingers work best for this. Put the pie pan into the freezer until the crust is frozen. Fill the frozen crust with about one pint of your homemade ice cream at the semihard stage. Complete freezing and serve as directed on page 150.

Vanilla Wafer Pie Crust

> **40** vanilla wafers (to make 1⅔ to 1¾ cups of fine crumbs)
> ¼ cup melted butter
> ¼ cup sugar

Follow the directions for making Graham Cracker Pie Crust.

Chocolate Wafer Pie Crust

> **20** or more chocolate wafers (to make 1⅔ to 1¾ cups of fine crumbs)
> ¼ cup melted butter
> ¼ cup sugar

The only problem is that chocolate wafers are not so standardized in size as graham crackers or vanilla wafers—20 wafers is an estimated starting point for making 1⅔ cups of crumbs. Follow the directions for making Graham Cracker Pie Crust.

Pastry Crust

1⅓ cups all-purpose flour
½ teaspoon salt
½ cup vegetable shortening
2 to 3 tablespoons water

Sift the flour, then measure 1⅓ cups. Put it into a bowl and mix in the salt. Lightly work in the shortening with a pastry blender or with your fingertips—it should make pea-size lumps. Sprinkle on 2 or 3 tablespoons of water and blend in lightly. Use just enough to hold the dough together. It's a good idea to chill the dough before rolling. Roll out the crust as little and as lightly as you can, and line a lightly buttered 9-inch pie pan with it. Prick the crust with a fork.

Put into a preheated 425-degree oven and bake for 10 to 15 minutes or until lightly browned.

Cool, then place the crust in the freezer for a few hours before filling it with your homemade ice cream.

Some suggestions:

1. Pumpkin Ice Cream with whipped cream.

2. Mint Ice Cream in a Chocolate Wafer Pie Crust.

3. Coffee Ice Cream with a chocolate sauce topping.

4. Chocolate Fudge Ice Cream bottom layer, topped with Joyce's Coffee Fudge Ice Cream.

ICE CREAM ROLLS

These look like jelly rolls, with ice cream substituted for the jelly, and they make impressive desserts.

All types of ice cream can be made into festive rolls. For the best visual effect, use a colorful ice cream with white cake and a light ice cream with the chocolate cake.

The cake: Use one of the following white or chocolate sponge cakes, as regular cake will not roll so well. For a cake pan we use a flat three-quart Pyrex dish (9 by 13 inches). If you happen to have a regular jelly roll pan, all the better. The finished hot cake is turned out onto a tea towel, rolled up and allowed to cool. This makes it easier to roll up again after filling.

To fill and roll the cake: Let the ice cream soften at room temperature for 10 or 15 minutes before using. If it is very hard, soften it a bit by pressing with the bottom of a large spoon—it must be just soft enough to spread.

Unroll the cooled cake and spread the ice cream evenly over the surface. Now roll up the cake again, lifting the tea towel under it to keep it rolled. Work gently to prevent tearing. Wrap the completed ice cream roll in foil or plastic wrap and place it in the freezer to harden.

To serve: Take out of the freezer and let stand at room temperature for 10 minutes before serving. You may want to garnish it with one of the ice cream sauces or an icing or fresh sliced fruit. Use a bread knife to slice it.

The following sponge cakes are simple to make, and each accommodates about a quart of ice cream to serve six or eight.

White Sponge Ice Cream Roll

> 3 eggs at room temperature
> ½ tablespoon lemon juice
> A few grains of salt
> ½ cup sugar
> ½ cup flour
> Powdered sugar

Preheat the oven to 325 degrees.

Prepare a 9- by 13-inch baking pan by lightly buttering it, then line with waxed paper and butter the paper. It is essential to have an easily removable cake to prevent tearing. We have good results using PAM on the waxed paper.

Put the eggs and lemon juice in a mixing bowl and beat at high speed for at least 10 minutes, preferably 15. This will greatly expand the eggs in volume and give the cake its light texture. Slow the mixer and gradually add the salt, sugar and flour. Beat only until mixed.

Pour the mix into the prepared baking pan. Put into the preheated 325-degree oven and bake for 20 to 25 minutes. The cake will be resilient when done and about ¼ inch high.

Have ready a tea towel sprinkled with powdered sugar. Immediately turn the pan over the towel and let the cake fall out. Peel the waxed paper off the cake; then roll the cake up in the towel, allowing it to cool.

When cool, spread the cake with slightly softened

ice cream and roll, freeze and serve as directed on
page 153.

Chocolate Sponge Ice Cream Roll

> 3 **eggs at room temperature**
> 1 **tablespoon instant cocoa**
> **A few grains of salt**
> ½ **cup sugar**
> ½ **cup flour**
> **Powdered sugar**

Preheat the oven to 325 degrees, and prepare a 9-
by 13-inch baking pan as directed for White Sponge
Ice Cream Roll.

Put the eggs and instant cocoa in a mixing bowl and
beat at high speed for at least 10 minutes, preferably
15. Then complete the recipe as directed for White
Sponge Ice Cream Roll.

ICE CREAM CAKES

Almost everyone likes ice cream with cake. When
you combine the two you have an unbeatable dessert.

Ice cream can be wedded with cake in several ways.
Just don't try baking ice cream inside the cake as we
did in one memorable experiment—the scientist in
the family thought that by using a very high temperature we could bake the cake before the ice cream
melted. We ended with a soggy-centered cake.

An 8- or 9-inch cake will accommodate about a quart
of ice cream between two layers and serve six to eight.
For more and thinner layers, spread the ice cream

more thinly—you'll need about 1½ pints to cover each of these thin layers.

Ice Cream Layer Cake

**1 8- or 9-inch cake
Icing (optional)
1 quart of ice cream**

Buy or bake your favorite cake and cut it into two or more layers. Make your icing and have it ready. Soften the ice cream as directed on page 153—it must be just soft enough to spread.

Spread the ice cream evenly between the cake layers. Quickly spread the icing on top and store in the freezer until dessert time.

To serve: Take out of the freezer and let stand at room temperature for 10 minutes before serving. Use a bread knife to slice it.

Old Hidden Ice Cream Cake

Bake your favorite cake in two 9-inch round cake pans, turning them out of the pans to cool. (Or buy two plain 9-inch cakes.)

Make your icing and have it ready.

Place the bottom layer of your cake on a serving plate. Use a saucer to mark a circle on the cake. Scoop out the cake within this circle and feed to hungry children. You now have an outer ring of cake for your bottom layer. Then carefully split the top layer with a bread knife, thus making two more layers. Put the bottom of these layers on top of the hollowed cake and cut a matching hole in it. This makes a nice chamber for the ice cream.

Soften the ice cream as directed on page 153 and pack it inside the double ring of cake. Cover with the intact top layer of cake. Quickly ice the entire cake and pop it into your freezer.

To serve: Take the ice cream cake out of the freezer and let it stand at room temperature for 10 minutes before serving. Use a bread knife—and each person gets a piece of ice cream in his cake.

Here are some good combinations:

1. Chocolate cake filled with Orange Sherbet.

2. Burnt sugar cake filled with Chocolate Ice Cream.

3. White cake filled with Coffee Fudge Ribbon Ice Cream.

4. Alternate layers of white and chocolate cake filled with Vanilla, Strawberry and Chocolate Ice Cream.

5. Banana cake filled with Chocolate Ice Cream.

Frozen Mousses
and Bombes

They say the best men are molded out of faults.
— SHAKESPEARE

MOUSSES

Frozen mousses resemble ice creams but are frozen without continuous stirring. They are valuable if you don't have an ice cream freezer, since you only use your refrigerator freezer. We find ice cream superior in taste and texture and use frozen mousses only when making bombes.

These mousse recipes make about one pint, and when used alone serve two to four.

Frozen Chocolate Mousse

1 egg
1 cup milk
¾ cup sugar
1 square (1 ounce) unsweetened chocolate
  A few grains of salt
½ teaspoon pure vanilla extract
1 cup heavy whipping cream

Break the egg into the top of a double boiler over simmering water, beat it slightly and then add the milk, sugar, chocolate and salt. Stir well as the chocolate melts. In about 10 minutes the mixture will thicken slightly and should be removed from the heat. Put into a bowl and cool, and then add the vanilla extract.

Pour in the whipping cream and beat until thick (5 to 10 minutes). To speed the freezing, put the small bowl into a larger bowl filled with ice chips. Then, as you beat, the cream mixture will chill and thicken more rapidly. (Use this technique with all mousses.)

If you're serving the mousse by itself, put into a serving dish, cover and put into the freezer until serving time. If you're using it in a bombe, just cover the bowl and put it in the freezer.

Frozen Coffee Mousse

2 tablespoons instant coffee
½ cup sugar
1 egg
1 cup milk
1 tablespoon Kahlúa liqueur (optional)
1 cup heavy whipping cream

Combine the coffee, sugar, egg and milk in the top of a double boiler over simmering water. Cook, then cool (add a tablespoon of Kahlúa liqueur if you like), beat in the heavy whipping cream and freeze as directed for Frozen Chocolate Mousse.

Frozen Praline Mousse

½ cup brown sugar
½ cup walnut pieces
2 eggs
2 tablespoons granulated sugar
A few grains of salt
1 cup milk
½ teaspoon pure vanilla extract
1 cup heavy whipping cream

Heat the brown sugar over moderate heat until it has melted (about 10 minutes). Watch carefully. Stir the walnuts into the syrup and pour onto waxed paper to cool. Then pulverize half of this candy by putting it in a plastic bag and rolling it with a rolling pin.

Break the eggs into the top of a double boiler over simmering water, beat slightly, then stir in the granulated sugar, the salt, the pulverized praline and milk. Cook, stirring, until it forms a custard thick enough to coat the spoon (about 10 minutes). Cool, and add the vanilla extract. Beat in the heavy whipping cream, stir in the remaining praline and freeze as directed for Frozen Chocolate Mousse.

Frozen Vanilla Mousse

1 egg
1 cup milk
⅓ cup sugar
A few grains of salt
1 tablespoon pure vanilla extract
1 cup heavy whipping cream

Break the egg into the top of a double boiler over simmering water and beat lightly for 2 minutes. Then stir in the milk, sugar and salt. Cook, stirring well, until the mixture thickens enough to coat the spoon. Cool and add the vanilla extract. Then beat in the heavy whipping cream and freeze as directed for Frozen Chocolate Mousse.

Frozen Orange Mousse

No cooking for this one.

1 6-ounce can frozen orange
   juice concentrate
2 tablespoons sugar
1 cup heavy whipping cream

Thaw the orange juice. Put it into a bowl with the sugar, then beat in the heavy whipping cream and freeze as directed for Frozen Chocolate Mousse.

Frozen Maple Mousse

Again, no cooking.

½ cup pure maple syrup
1 cup milk
1 cup heavy whipping cream
¼ cup chopped walnuts (optional)

Just put the maple syrup into a bowl and stir in the milk. Then beat in the heavy whipping cream and freeze as directed for Frozen Chocolate Mousse.

If you like, you can stir in some chopped walnuts before freezing.

BOMBES

A bombe is a molded frozen dessert combining a mousse with ice cream or sherbet. Usually a layer of ice cream forms the outside covering, with a center of mousse inside it. Bombes make impressive desserts with their showy form and color contrast. With a little practice you'll make a perfect bombe.

For the bombe mold: Special bombe molds are available, but a metal or ceramic mixing bowl will work satisfactorily. Before starting the recipe, put the mold into the freezer to chill. Unmolding later will be much easier if you spray the inside of the mold with PAM.

To make the bombe: First assemble the components. Prepare the mousse and freeze it to semihard. The ice cream should also be semihard and of spreadable consistency. If you've made it earlier, take it out of the freezer and let stand at room temperature for 10 minutes, then soften it by pressing with the bottom of a large spoon.

Scoop the ice cream into the chilled mold, spreading it to an even thickness all over the surface. Work quickly before the ice cream melts. Then fill up the center with the mousse and replace in the refrigerator freezer. Freeze until completely hard—at least six hours.

To unmold: Unmold, using a hot damp cloth as directed on page 144. If your bombe is well frozen and the mold well lubricated, the bombe will neatly exit the mold. Quickly replace the bombe in the freezer. If you won't be serving it for several hours, cover lightly with waxed paper.

To serve: Take out of the freezer and let stand at room temperature for a few minutes before serving. To cut, use a cake knife and dip it into hot water before cutting.

A six-cup bombe mold is the size for the bombes described here. All use one quart of ice cream and one pint of mousse. They easily serve eight, and can serve up to twelve.

Some suggestions:

1. Frozen Chocolate Mousse center, covered with any of these ice creams : Vanilla, Coffee, Mint, Pistachio, Banana, Butter Pecan, or Orange Sherbet.

2. Frozen Coffee Mousse center, covered with one of the following ice creams: Vanilla, Chocolate, Mint, Rum Raisin or Chocolate Fudge Ribbon.

3. Frozen Praline Mousse center, covered with one of the following ice creams: Vanilla, Chocolate, Coffee, Pumpkin, or Orange Sherbet.

4. Frozen Vanilla Mousse center, covered with one of the following ice creams: Chocolate, Coffee, Peach, Butterscotch or Peppermint Stick, or Cranberry or Mango Sherbet.

5. Frozen Orange Mousse center, covered with one of the following ice creams: Chocolate, Vanilla, Banana, Rum Raisin, or any sherbet.

6. Frozen Maple Mousse center, covered with Lime Sherbet, or with one of the following ice creams: Chocolate Fudge Ribbon, Chocolate, Coffee, Peach, or Pumpkin.